To Colonel

Ferment!

Fermentation for Beginners

Text © Rachel Mulligan
Design and photography © Pipin`s book 2018

Editor: Mina Mušinović
Copy Editor: Jeff Bickert
Photography: Rachel Mulligan, Mina Mušinović, Ksenija Konvalinka
Shutterstock (see page 159 for additional credits)
Illustrations: Ksenija Konvalinka
Design: Ksenija Konvalinka

A CIP catalog record for this book is available from the Library of Congress and the British Library.

ISBN 978-0-9956314-1-0
Printed in Slovenia

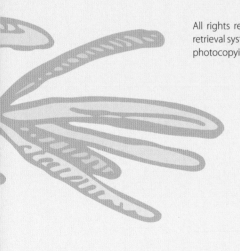

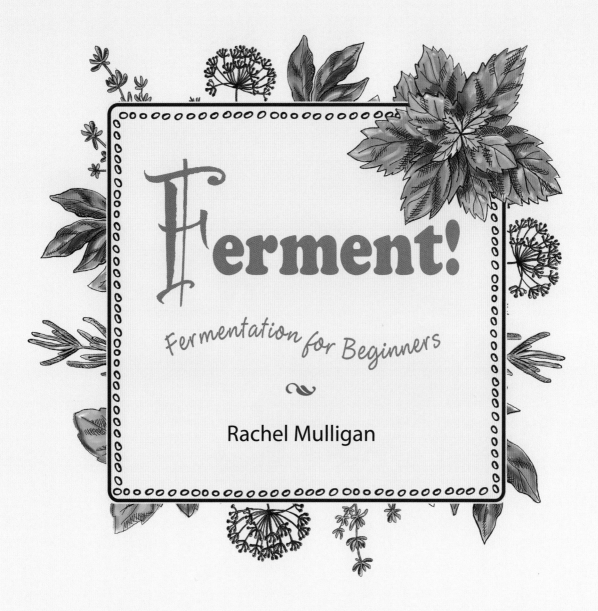

Ferment!

Fermentation for Beginners

❧

Rachel Mulligan

Acknowledgements

My warmest thanks and gratitude go to my best friend Pauline MacRonald, who helped fashion the direction of the book and provided many insightful ideas. She has also proven herself an eager taste-tester, happy to try even my most unusual of concoctions!

Thanks to my husband Peter for his support throughout the time it took for me to write the book. He is slowly coming round to the importance of fermented foods in his diet – not that I nag him much about it!

To Cathal, my number one fan and a great lover of my spicy napa cabbage kimchi recipe.

Thanks Mina M for your insight, expertise and guidance throughout this process.

A special thanks is extended to Vital Veg, Inverurie, who provide me with the most wonderful local and seasonal organic vegetables.

… and last but not least, thank you dear reader for choosing this book to help you begin your journey into the world of fermenting.

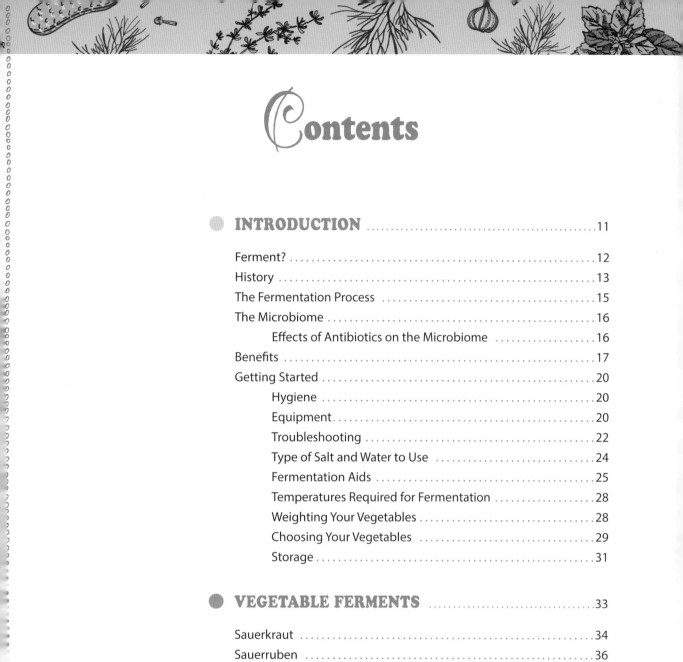

Contents

Introduction

Ferment?

What's the first thing that comes to mind at the mention of cultured foods? Perhaps you picked this book up because you've noticed the growing interest in fermented foods and their many potential health benefits? Maybe you have already had a go at experimenting on your own, but would like to improve your knowledge and expand your range. Whatever the reason, I have created "Ferment!" as a beginner's guide to help you get started on your journey.

This book will help you to learn the basics of fermentation as well as improve your understanding of the numerous health benefits that this ancient method of preserving food can bring when enjoyed as part of your daily diet.

I have collected my favourite tried-and-tested recipes for fermenting fruits, vegetables, grains and dairy for you to try.

Rachel Mulligan

Key

  Very easy

   Easy (takes time to prepare)

    Moderate (can be tricky and/or time consuming)

History

No one really knows how people learnt the skill of fermenting, but it seems likely that it was discovered by accident when foods were left for a period of time, allowing fermentation to begin naturally. Once it was discovered that fermentation both preserved the food and was delicious, people refined their skills and fermentation methods began to improve.

The use of fermentation, particularly for drinks (ethanol-based ferments, i.e. alcohol), has been around since Neolithic times and has been documented from 7000–6600 BC in the ancient town of Jiahu, China. Sorghum beer dates back to pre-historic times and is still made throughout Africa today. However, numerous records point to widespread use around the world some thousands of years ago.

Fermentations that produce ethanol are some of the oldest known to humankind. A common method still used by some cultures even today, even if it does not sound terribly appetizing, is the chewing of grains to induce the hydrolysis of starches. The grain is then sundried and thereafter mixed with water before being left to ferment with wild yeasts. Some examples of beverages that employed chewing in the initial phases of production are *chicha* corn beer from the Andes region of South America and Japanese sake.

A sorghum field. In many regions in Africa sorghum grains are still fermented to make beer.

Sweet half sake. Up until the 1930s, sake was still being made made in some parts of Japan by first chewing cooked rice before spitting it into a container. The resulting liquid was then left to ferment.

It is believed that without fermentation, which not only preserves food but makes it easier to digest, humankind would have struggled to survive.

Fermentation can actually make a food that would otherwise be toxic safe for human consumption, such as *garri*. This is a West African ferment made from the root vegetable cassava, which contains natural cyanides. Fermenting causes chemical changes that neutralise the toxin. But not only does fermenting help make certain foods safe to eat, some ferments are even considered natural remedies – so much so that they are used in medicines to fight certain illnesses. A good example is the Tanzanian *togwa*, a drink made from fermented gruel, which has been found to protect the body against food-borne illnesses in regions were sanitation is poor.

Groud cassava, used to make the West African ferment *garri*. Fermentation causes chemical changes that make cassava safe for human consumption.

There are numerous examples of fermented food found all over the world. Perhaps some of the most well known and popular are *miso* or fermented bean pastes from Japan and Korea, *kisla repa*, shredded turnip from the Balkan region, *nem chua*, fermented pork from Vietnam, and *şalgam*, a fermented drink from Turkey usually made from purple carrot and bulgur.

Traditional Turkish Şalgam.

Coffee beans during fermentation.

And the fact is, we all eat fermented foods, even if we aren't entirely aware of it. For example, chocolate, coffee, yoghurt, sour cream, olives, soy sauce, cheese and vinegar are all fermented.

The Fermentation Process

During vegetable fermentation beneficial microbes convert glucose into lactic acid, along with smaller amounts of ethanol and carbon dioxide.

Generally, the entire process is started by the bacteria *Leuconostoc mesenteroides*, which raises the acidity of a brine to 0.3 %. As the acidity continues to rise the *Leuconostoc* begin to die and *Lactobacillus plantarum* take over, bringing the acidity up to 2 %. The optimum temperature for bacteria, active in the fermentation process is between 15 and 22°C.

Lactic acid bacteria thrive in acidic, salty, anaerobic environments and win the race for the nutrients found in these conditions. As a result, they effectively inhibit the growth of other microorganisms. Lactic acid bacteria are found in a variety of environments, including the surface of vegetables.

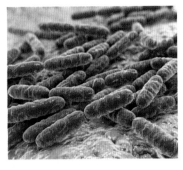

Lactobacillus, lactic acid bacteria, part of the normal flora of the human gut.

Of course there are thousands of other types of microbes found on the surface of vegetables even after thorough washing. In order for fermentation to progress successfully it is therefore imperative to ensure conditions are most favourable for the lactic acid bacteria, allowing them to multiply rapidly.

In order for fermentation to be both safe and work well the vegetables should be submerged in a salty brine of between 1 and 3 % salinity.

The Microbiome

The human body is home to around 100 trillion microbes in the form of bacteria, viruses, archaea and fungi. That's ten times the number of microbial cells for each human cell. Collectively, this community of microbes is known as the microbiome.

We often think of microbes as harmful, when in fact only a small fraction of the millions of species are harmful to humans. Indeed, many are essential to our good health, as they assist in metabolic processes and help support our immune system.

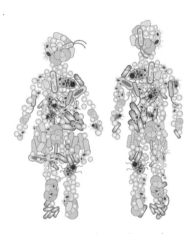

The human microbiome. Researchers from all over the world have taken part in the *Human Microbiome Project (HMP)*. It is hoped the research will help to clarify the role of microbes in illnesses and in maintaining good health.

Research is beginning to show that if our microbiome has been depleted we are at risk of developing conditions such as acne, depression, autism, obesity, diabetes, IBS, allergies and auto-immune diseases. It would appear that the modern diet, chemicals in our environment and antibiotics could all play a role in reducing the biodiversity of important microbes in the gut.

Effects of Antibiotics on the Microbiome ○○○○○○○

Antibiotics are lifesaving drugs, and sometimes their use is absolutely necessary. Diseases that would have killed us in the past can now be effectively treated using antibiotics.

It is worth bearing in mind, however, that antibiotics can be indiscriminate, killing off all types of bacteria, good and bad. The more broad-spectrum (non-specific) the antibiotic the more damage can be caused to the mix of beneficial bacteria in the gut microbiome.

Damage caused can be long term, with studies showing that the microbiome can take up to a full year to recover from some types of antibiotics.

Consuming fermented foods during and after taking a course of antibiotics can help your gut to recover more quickly. Cultured foods can help repopulate the gut and crowd out any less desirable bacteria.

Benefits

Fermented foods are full of beneficial bacteria that can supply our guts with essential living bacteria. This helps to maintain a gut microbiome rich in diversity. Fermented foods can contain many times more beneficial microbes than a probiotic supplement. A diverse microbiome is linked to a better immune system by improving gut health. A healthy gut rich in probiotics produces antibiotic, antitumor, antiviral and

A sample of fermented food, great for supporting gut health. From top left: kimchi, apple cider vinegar. From middle left: crème fraîche, red beets. From bottom left: cucumber, sauerkraut.

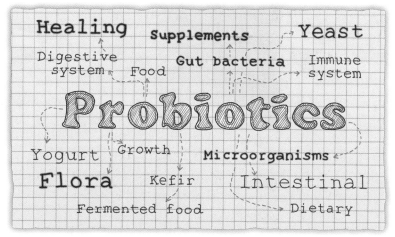

antifungal substances. Also, the acids in fermented food make a healthy gut a hostile environment for pathogens.

A healthy gut is also better able to extract nutrients from the food we consume.

Some bacteria are able to increase the nutritional value of food through fermentation, especially the B vitamins. And vitamin K2, also found in fermented food, has been attributed to helping prevent the build-up of plaque on artery walls.

Health benefits of vitamins and minerals.

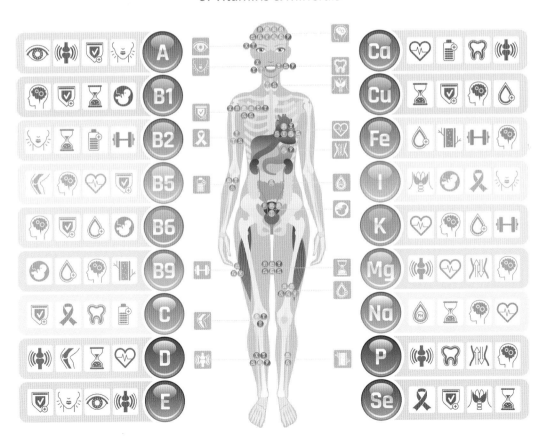

VITAMINS Health Benefits MINERALS
of vitamins & minerals

The process of fermentation makes raw ingredients easier to digest by making the vitamins and minerals in our food more easily available for absorption in our digestive system. By consuming fermented foods, we are increasing the amount of vitamins B and C in our systems immensely. Vitamin C plays a vital role in maintaining collagen production and bone health, while B-12 is essential for the development and function of red blood cells and the correct function of the nervous system.

Other vitamins that are similarly enhanced during fermentation include: thiamin (B1) and niacin (B3) which maintain good metabolic and nervous system health; folic acid, which plays a role in red blood cell production; riboflavin (vitamin B2) for good skin, eyes and nervous system; and biotin (B7) which metabolises fat. The probiotics (good bacteria), enzymes (biological catalysts) and lactic acid allow the vitamins and minerals to be more easily absorbed into the body.

Fermented foods provide enzymes necessary for digestion. Cooked food has no enzymes, while raw food has some, but fermented food is abundant in enzymes.

Some foods contain what are sometimes referred to as "anti-nutrients", such as phytic acid found in grains, beans and seeds, or synthetic compounds that have entered the food chain. Some scientists believe that phytic acid is responsible for lowering the bioavailability of important nutrients such as iron and zinc. These "anti-nutrients" can be destroyed through fermentation by allowing important nutrients to be absorbed by the body. But phytic acid is not all bad, and recent research seems to suggest it may help combat various types of cancer.

The outer layer of grains and beans contains phytic acid, which is responsible for lowering the bioavailability of some nutrients. Soaking the grains and beans before cooking releases the phytic acid into the water, which is why we always drain grains and beans before further use.

Microbes in the fermentation process are able to break down the otherwise indigestible cellulose found in plant foods, making them more digestible. In milk ferments such as yoghurt and kefir the lactose is used by the microbes as a source of

food. This results in a food very low in lactose, which may also be eaten by those with lactose intolerance.

Fermented food is also credited with effectively detoxifying various heavy metals and toxins.

Getting Started

Hygiene ∘∘∘∘∘∘∘∘∘∘∘∘∘∘∘∘∘∘∘∘∘∘∘∘∘∘∘∘∘∘∘∘∘∘∘∘∘∘

It is important to ensure all your utensils are clean before you begin. It is sufficient to wash everything in hot soapy water and then rinse thoroughly.

The fermentation process kills off pathogenic microbes; but if your utensils are not properly clean before you begin, unwanted microbes may get a foothold in your ferment and cause it to go off.

Also, ensure your hands have been washed thoroughly before you begin.

Equipment ∘∘∘∘∘∘∘∘∘∘∘∘∘∘∘∘∘∘∘∘∘∘∘∘∘∘∘∘∘∘∘∘∘∘∘∘

You really don't need any special equipment to start fermenting. All you need to get started is a non-reactive bowl (food grade plastic or glass) and some glass jars and bottles with lids. Glass jars with clamp-down fastening schemes such as Kilner and Mason jars are ideal but not essential.

It is best to use non-reactive equipment because the fermentation process creates an acidic environment and the acids may react with metal or plastics, causing chemicals to leach into the ferment.

Ferments such as kombucha and kefir require mothers or starter cultures. If you know someone who makes these ferments, they can pass on some culture to you; if not, you can buy them online.

Basic equipment for fermenting.

Some examples of the types of jars and bottles that can be used for fermenting and storage.

Troubleshooting ⚬⚬⚬⚬⚬⚬⚬⚬⚬⚬⚬⚬⚬⚬⚬⚬⚬⚬⚬⚬⚬⚬⚬⚬⚬⚬⚬⚬⚬⚬⚬

Sometimes, despite your best efforts, things can go wrong with your ferment. You might notice an obvious fluffy or coloured mould on top or a thin cloudy film of yeast – so what do you do?

Remember to clean your equipment thoroughly and ensure your vegetables are always kept submerged below the level of the brine.

Use fresh vegetables – older vegetables may have high concentration of undesirable moulds which may gain a foothold in your ferment before the beneficial microbes reach sufficient volume and the fermenting medium is sufficiently acidic.

Use the right amount of salt in your brine to ensure the right conditions develop to feed the good microbes and discourage the less desirable ones.

Mould on a fruit ferment.

∾ Moulds

There are so many differing opinions on how to treat mould on your ferment from scooping out any visible mould from the top to discarding the whole ferment.

I always discard mouldy ferments in the compost.

Mould on fermented berries.

Mould on a vegetable ferment.

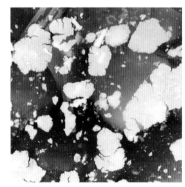

White fungi and mould floating on surface of fermented tomatoes.

Mould is usually found on top of the ferment and may manifest itself as fuzzy blue, green, or white spots. Mould is the visible sporing body of the microbe but most of the microbe may be invisibly penetrating the entire ferment. When you see mould on top of your ferment your entire ferment is likely contaminated.

Of course some moulds are safe to eat, such as those found in some cheeses and tempeh, but unless you are an expert microbiologist it is best to err on the side of caution and entirely discard a mouldy ferment. Many moulds are toxic.

Kahm Yeast

Kahm yeast manifests as a thin cloudy film on top of the ferment and there can be air bubbles trapped beneath. Kahm yeast growth can occur if the medium is insufficiently acidic, the conditions are too warm or not enough salt was added to the mixture. It has a yeasty or cheesy aroma and although harmless it can impart an unpleasant taste to the ferment.

Kham yeast can be skimmed from the top of your ferment, but if the conditions have encouraged the growth of kham yeast in the first place you may find it continues to be a problem. If this is the case then just use the ferment up quickly.

Close-up of kahm yeast on surface of cucumber ferment.

Type of Salt and Water to Use ◦◦◦◦◦◦◦◦◦◦◦◦◦◦◦◦◦◦◦◦

From top: French sea salt, Himalayan pink salt and Cornish sea salt.

Although fermentation can be carried out without salt, the addition of salt will help prevent vegetables from going mushy. Salt also enhances flavours and inhibits the growth of competing, less desirable bacteria, allowing the salt-tolerant, beneficial bacteria from genus *Lactobacillus* to flourish.

The more salt added to the ferment the slower the fermentation process and vice versa. In general, two tablespoons of salt should be sufficient for two kilograms of vegetables, but more or less can be added according to individual tastes.

It is important to get the volume of salt correct when fermenting, otherwise there is potential for less favourable microbes to get a foothold. Ensuring vegetables are completely submerged reduces the chance of surface moulds destroying the ferment.

Use sea salt, rock salt or pink Himalayan salt, as these contain trace elements and do not contain anti-caking agents or other additives. Table salt contains additives that may inhibit the growth of the beneficial microbes required for successful fermentation.

Some recipes require dry salting to draw water out of the vegetable, such as sauerkraut and kimchi. Cabbage holds a lot of water, and when salt is added it creates its own brine solution. Other recipes require the salt to be dissolved in water before adding it to the vegetable.

Celery juice and seaweed can also be used in fermentation, but they will not prevent vegetables from going mushy.

Where possible, use filtered water for fermentation, as tap water contains chlorine that may inhibit or destroy beneficial microbes.

Raw honey can be used to ferment; however, a large volume is required and this makes it expensive.

Raw honey can be used when fermenting instead of brine.

Fermentation Aids ०००००००००००००००००००००००००००००००००

⌇ Kefir Grains (mother)

Kefir can be milk- or water-based and is a fermented drink produced by adding a symbiotic mix of yeast and bacteria commonly known as kefir grains. Kefir grains contain proteins, polysaccharides and variety of microorganisms, which produce lactic acid and have beneficial effect on the human organism.

Milk kefir grains.

If you wish to take a break from making milk kefir, then the grains can be stored in the fridge. Each teaspoon of kefir grains needs about 300 ml of full fat milk per week. Store the kefir in a covered jar or glass and change out the milk weekly to ensure there is sufficient food to keep the grains healthy.

When you are ready to begin fermenting again you will need to reactivate the grains. Leave the glass containing the grains out overnight, then discard the milk the following morning and place the grains in fresh milk. You will need to do this for several days until you notice the milk starting to thicken. Once the kefir grains are active again you can begin to use them again as normal.

Water kefir can be stored and reactivated in a similar manner, but instead of storing the grains in milk, water kefir grains should be stored in sugary water – about a tablespoon of sugar per 300 ml of water.

Water kefir grains.

There are communities of people online who are happy to give away their excess starter cultures. At kefirhood you can advertise that you have excess grains to give away for free or make contact with someone in your area who has grains to share (https://kefirhood.com/).

✎ Whey

Whey is a by-product obtained from curdled milk. During this process the casein protein and the majority of milk fats are separated, which results in whey being almost fat free but still rich in nutrients. It contains potassium, minerals and a large number of beneficial amino acids.

Whey can be used in the fermentation of fruits. The high sugar content of fruits can cause mould to grow before enough beneficial microbes have formed to start preservation. Using whey introduces beneficial microbes in large numbers, thus reducing the chances of undesirable microbes taking over and causing the ferment to go off.

Whey is a by-product obtained from curdled milk.

The whey can then be used straight away as a starter culture or refrigerated until ready to use, where it will keep for a couple of weeks. If using whey for fermentation it should be used as soon as possible, when the microbial population is at its highest.

You can make kefir whey yourself. More about how to make it appears under the Kefir Cheese recipe.

✎ Kombucha SCOBY (Symbiotic Culture of Bacteria and Yeast) (mother)

Kombucha is a fermented tea-based drink believed to have originated in the Far East, probably in China, where it has been drunk for at least 2000 years.

In order to make Kombucha a SCOBY is required. This is a community of bacteria and yeast held together by sticky cellulose produced by the bacteria.

SCOBYs are known by other names such as pellicle, mother, and mushroom (though it is not actually a mushroom), to name but a few. They generally contain the bacteria from genus *Gluconacetobacter*, *Acetobacter* and *Zygosaccharomyces* (along with other bacteria and yeasts).

SCOBY – Symbiotic culture of bacteria and yeast.

SCOBYs can be purchased online or passed on from one kombucha brewer to the next. Each time a batch of kombucha is fermented, a new SCOBY forms on top of the brew. Old SCOBYs can be composted, kept as a spare (stored in some of the kombucha liquid) or passed on to friends.

The procedure for storing a kombucha SCOBY is similar to that for kefir. Place the SCOBY in a clean jar and cover with kombucha liquid. Cover the jar and place it in a cool dark place until ready to reactivate. It may take a few brews of fresh kombucha to full reactivate the SCOBY.

A kombucha SCOBY can be stored for months in this manner and will be good to use as long as there are no visible mould patches. If mould is evident the SCOBY will have to be discarded and a new uncontaminated one obtained.

Kombucha and water kefir may be used as starters in some recipes.

Freeze-Dried Starter Cultures

These cultures accelerate the beginning of the fermentation process. Once the process is underway the naturally present microbes progress the fermentation.

Freeze-dried starter cultures contain only the most common fermentation bacteria and yeasts such as those found in kefir.

Try and find a brand that contains bacteria naturally found in the soil (this should be highlighted on the packaging) and follow the instructions on the packaging.

You will find freeze-dried starter cultures in good health food stores or online stores such as Amazon and similar.

Temperatures Required for Fermentation

Generally speaking, fermentation will proceed faster in warmer temperatures and slower in cooler temperatures.

I generally ferment at a room temperature of roughly 19° C; however, fermentation will progress successfully from 10° C upwards. If fermenting at lower temperatures, bear in mind that it may take up to six months for fermentation to complete.

Longer ferments can produce more complex flavours.

Weighting Your Vegetables

For your fermentation to be successful it is essential that the ingredients are fully submerged, as floating particles may encourage mould growth.

If you are adding herbs, add them to the bottom of the jar before adding heavier ingredients on top in order to reduce the chance of particles floating to the top.

During fermentation it is essential that the whole ferment remains submerged throughout the process.

You may wish to use a weight to keep your mixture submerged. I sometimes use a small jar (small enough to fit into the opening of the fermenting vessel) filled with brine to weigh down my ferment.

Glass and ceramic weights can be bought online, but ensure they are food safe.

I have read that some people use clean stones as a fermentation weight, but because ferments are acidic I

would be concerned about possible leaching from the stone into the ferment.

If you are fermenting tomatoes or other fruits and vegetables that float naturally, ensure you stir the mixture a couple of times a day to prevent mould growth. These tend to be shorter ferments, so mould is less of an issue here.

Choosing your vegetables

In order for fermentation to be successful it is necessary that beneficial microbes are present.

Non-organic vegetables from the supermarket have generally been coated in a preserving solution to kill off microbes so that the food will stay "fresh" longer.

Organic vegetables.

Example of organic garden on recycled raised beds.

Organic vegetables from the supermarket have generally had all soil removed and thereafter been washed in a mild saline solution for the same reason.

Organic vegetables bought from a local farmer still have soil present and therefore an abundance of beneficial microbes.

Of course, soil contains pathogenic microbes too, so it is therefore essential that the vegetables are washed thoroughly in cold water. This dilutes the microbial populations on the vegetable surface while still leaving enough beneficial microbes for successful fermentation. During fermentation, vegetables are often placed in a brine solution, which further inhibits the undesirable microbes and gives the beneficial microbes time to outnumber and overcome them.

I have used non-organic, supermarket organic and farm-fresh organic vegetables and have always managed to ferment successfully. I get most of my vegetables from a local organic farm. These vegetables are grown locally, are high-quality, pesticide-free and seasonal.

Studies have shown that fermenting vegetables may help remove any pesticides still present, effectively de-toxing the vegetable.

Storage

Most vegetable ferments can be kept in the fridge for up to nine months.

Fruit ferments tend to go off faster due to the higher sugar content and should generally be consumed within a month or two.

The best place to store your finished ferments is in the fridge, as the fermentation process continues at a far slower pace in a cool/cold environment.

Jars can also be stored in a cold dark place.

Larder shelf full of ferments.

Vegetable Ferments

Sauerkraut

This delicious ferment is well known and believed to have its origins in China. However, when it was brought to Europe about 1000 years ago the Germans altered the process from a rice wine ferment to a dry cure ferment.

In parts of Europe, especially the Balkan region, large-scale fermentation of cabbage is commonplace. The method used is exactly the same, but quantities of ingredients are scaled up accordingly.

It contains some B vitamins and is an excellent source of vitamin C, which is essential in helping maintain a healthy immune system; it may also help to lower cholesterol levels.

Method

1. Chop the cabbage into quarters and remove the core from each segment.

2. Thinly slice the cabbage and place it in a large non-reactive bowl. Add the caraway seeds and salt and massage the cabbage to ensure even distribution.

3. Leave to sit covered with a clean tea towel for about an hour to allow the cabbage to soften and release some of its juices.

4. After an hour pack the cabbage into a litre jar, compacting it firmly with your fist.

5. Add a heavy food-safe weight to the jar and close the lid. If you do not have a heavy weight then check the sauerkraut each day, and using a clean spoon to push down the cabbage ensure it remains thoroughly submerged in the brine.

6. The brine should begin to rise covering the cabbage over the next 24 hours. If there is insufficient brine to cover the cabbage then make up a brine solution of 1 tbsp of salt to 1 litre of filtered water and add enough to cover the cabbage.

7. Leave at room temperature and out of direct sunlight. After about two weeks you can taste the sauerkraut, but it can take up to six weeks to finish fermenting. You will see the cabbage turn more translucent, and any bubbles will stop rising.

Ingredients

- 1 small head of white cabbage (about 1 kg)
- 1 tsp caraway seeds
- 1½ tbsp salt
- 1 litre jar with lid

Top Tips

- You can of course use red cabbage, which is also very delicious. You may find that you will need to add extra brine to this.
- I like to add a couple of tablespoons of sauerkraut to my lunch salad. It also works well as a topping on burgers and hot dogs or in cheese sandwiches.
- To make delicious coleslaw that is both prebiotic and probiotic, just shred or grate 450 g of white or red cabbage along with one small carrot and one small red onion. Add two tablespoons of sauerkraut and a tablespoon of sour cream or mayonnaise.

Sauerruben

Sauerruben is very similar to sauerkraut, but instead of using cabbage we use turnips.

This ferment is very popular throughout Eastern Europe and Balkan region, where it is used in traditional recipes and large-scale fermentation of turnip is commonplace. The method used is exactly the same, but quantities are scaled up accordingly.

Turnips are high in fibre, phytonutrients and antioxidants and have a beneficial anti-inflammatory effect on the body. They are also high in the B vitamin folate, which is essential for heart health, as well as in vitamins C, A and E, manganese, calcium, potassium and beta-carotene.

Method

1. Shred the turnip and place in a large non-reactive bowl. Add the cloves and salt and massage the turnip mixture to ensure even distribution.

2. Leave to sit covered with a clean tea towel for about an hour to allow the turnip to soften and release some of its juices.

3. After an hour pack the turnip mixture into a litre jar, compacting it firmly with your fist.

4. Add a heavy food-safe weight to the jar and close the lid. If you do not have a heavy weight then check the jar each day, and using a clean spoon push down the turnip ensuring it remains submerged in the brine.

5. The brine should begin to rise, covering the turnip over the next 24 hours. If there is insufficient brine to cover the turnip then make up a brine solution of 1 tbsp of salt to 1 litre of filtered water and add enough to cover the turnip.

6. Leave at room temperature and out of direct sunlight. After about two weeks you can taste the sauerruben. Once it is soured to your liking refrigerate.

Ingredients

- 1 turnip (about 1 kg)
- 4 cloves
- 3 crushed black peppercorns
- 1½ tbsp salt
- 1 litre jar with lid

Cloves give aroma and flavour.

Top Tips

- Sauerruben can be used in the same way as sauerkraut.
- It also makes a great addition to a hearty bean soup: fry some onion and garlic until lightly browned, then add some vegetable stock and a tin of mixed beans. Heat through. Add a few tablespoons of sauerruben near the end of the cooking and serve with some chopped chives.

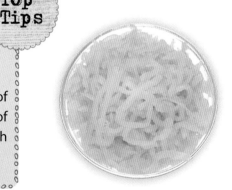

Brusselskraut

This easy recipe is a great way to get the nutritious, often overlooked Brussels sprout into your seasonal diet.

Brussels sprouts are high in vitamins and fibre, and are even more nutritious once fermented.

They are an excellent source of vitamin C and vitamin K, and a very good source of other nutrients including potassium, vitamins B1 and B6, manganese, choline, copper, phosphorus and omega-3 fatty acids.

Method

1. Wash the Brussels sprouts well, removing any damaged outer leaves.

2. Slice the sprouts finely and place in a large non-reactive bowl. Add salt, caraway seeds and freshly ground black pepper and mix well together.

3. Cover and leave for a few hours to allow the salt to draw the juices out of the sprouts.

4. Pack the mixture into a litre jar ensuring it is well compacted.

5. If there is insufficient brine to cover the sprouts then make up a brine of about 1 tsp of salt in 250 ml of water and top up until covered. Ensure the mixture is submerged, close the lid and leave for about 4 weeks.

Ingredients

- 1 kg Brussels sprouts
- 1 tbsp salt
- ½ tsp caraway seeds
- ½ tsp freshly ground black pepper
- 1 litre jar with lid

Top Tips

- Brussels sprouts are most commonly consumed around Christmas time. If you make this ferment a few weeks before Christmas it will add festive cheer to a cold leftover turkey sandwich along with a little cranberry relish.
- I like to sprinkle fermented Brussels sprouts onto salads – add some pomegranate, slices of orange, maybe a sprinkle of cinnamon and you have a wonderful salad that is Christmassy and healthy!
- Of course it can also be used as you would sauerkraut or sauerruben.

Fermented Carrots

This recipe couldn't be easier, and has the added benefit of being packed with the beneficial probiotics produced during the fermentation process.

Carrots are not only delicious but they can help improve vision, have anti-cancer properties, and the beta-carotene found in carrots slows the aging process.

And according to a Harvard University study, people who ate five or more carrots a week were less likely to suffer a stroke than those who did not.

Method

1. Wash the carrots, paying special attention to the soil that could be stuck in some of the furrows. Remove the tops and tails before cutting into batons.

2. Peel the garlic and place it in the bottom of a litre jar, then pack the carrot batons vertically into the jar as tightly together as possible.

3. Dissolve the salt into the water and pour over the carrots.

4. Close the jar and leave to ferment for up to two weeks at room temperature.

5. Taste after one week and refrigerate once the carrots have soured to your taste.

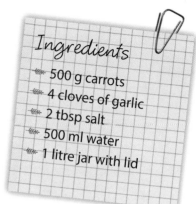

Ingredients

- 500 g carrots
- 4 cloves of garlic
- 2 tbsp salt
- 500 ml water
- 1 litre jar with lid

Top Tips

- To make a healthy lunch box snack, make a quick and easy hummus. Add a tin of chickpeas, a clove of garlic (why not use fermented garlic?), the juice of half a lemon and the rind of a quarter-lemon into a blender. Add a tablespoon of tahini (sesame seed paste), a tablespoon of olive oil and whizz until smooth. Use the fermented carrot batons to dip into the hummus.

Fermented Green Beans

Although this is an easy ferment I have given it a two-cabbage rating, as it is especially important to use only fresh beans and that they are kept submerged to avoid spots of white mould.

Green beans are a great source of fibre, vitamins A, C, K, B6, and folic acid. In terms of minerals, green beans are a good source of calcium, silicon, iron, manganese, potassium, and copper.

Method

1. Thoroughly wash the beans, making sure you only keep the good, completely fresh ones. Cut off all the ends.

2. Peel and slice or grate the garlic.

3. Crush the peppercorns using a mortar and pestle, if you have one. Alternatively, you will get the same results crushing the peppercorns in a bowl with a heavy-based glass, or any other way that works.

4. Add the beans, garlic, dill or mint and peppercorns to a 500 ml jar.

5. Dissolve the salt in the water and cover the bean mixture.

6. Close the jar and leave to ferment at room temperature for up to two weeks.

7. Refrigerate.

Ingredients

- 225 g green beans
- 2 cloves of garlic
- sprig of dill or mint
- 4 peppercorns
- 1½ tbsp salt
- 250 ml water
- 500 ml jar with lid

Top Tips

- This makes a vibrant addition to *tabbouleh*. Cook 50 g bulgur wheat and set aside to drain and cool. Chop 50 g each of parsley and mint and add to a bowl. Add 200 g of chopped tomatoes, 50 g of chopped fermented green beans, 3 chopped spring onions, the juice of 1 lemon, and 3 tbsp olive oil. Stir in the bulgur wheat and enjoy.

Fermented Asparagus

Asparagus is an excellent prebiotic, which means when eaten it provides beneficial gut bacteria with a source of food that helps them to thrive. Asparagus also contains vitamins A, B and C.

It is a versatile seasonal vegetable. Make the most of it when it is in season and in plentiful supply by fermenting a few batches.

Method

1. Wash the asparagus and remove any woody ends. Chop the spears diagonally into 5 cm lengths.

2. Add mustard seeds, bay leaf and asparagus to a litre jar.

3. Dilute salt in 600 ml of water and cover the contents with the brine, ensuring all the ingredients are submerged.

4. Close the lid and leave at room temperature for about 2 weeks.

5. After the asparagus have reached the desired sourness, refrigerate.

Ingredients

- 15 spears of asparagus
- 1 tbsp mustard seeds
- 1 bay leaf
- 1 tbsp salt
- 600 ml water
- 1 litre jar with lid

Top Tips

- Fermented asparagus is delicious just as it is, but it is highly versatile and can be used in salads and sandwiches.
- Try chopping 200 g of fermented asparagus into thin slices and place in a medium bowl. Add one finely chopped red onion, 125 g of grated pecorino cheese, 120 ml of apple cider vinegar (use you own fermented vinegar if you have any) and 3 tbsp of olive oil. Mix well and leave to sit for about an hour before serving.

Fermented Garlic

This is such an easy and delicious way to preserve garlic. I have given this easy recipe a three-cabbage rating because preparing the garlic cloves is time consuming.

Research has shown that blood pressure and cholesterol levels can be lowered by consuming 3–5 g of garlic per day. It can also help to minimise the risk of arteriosclerosis, which is implicated in heart attacks and strokes. Fermenting garlic increases the bioavailability of its nutrients and the amount of antioxidants.

Method

1. Peel each clove of garlic and add to a litre jar.

2. Dissolve the salt in 600 ml of water and pour over the garlic.

3. Leave to ferment at room temperature for several weeks. You will have to open the jar briefly every day to release any built-up gas.

4. The fermentation process is complete once bubbles stop forming. At this point the jar is ready to be refrigerated.

Ingredients

- 12 bulbs of garlic
- 2 tbsp salt
- 600 ml water
- 1 litre jar with lid

Add some finely-chopped chilli to add a little heat.

Top Tips

- It is normal for some or all of the cloves to turn blue or green. The garlic is still delicious and still perfectly safe to eat.
- The fermented garlic can be used like you would in any of your favourite recipes, chopped finely and added to salads, or used to add probiotic goodness to guacamole.
- To make guacamole, finely chop one or two cloves of fermented garlic. Remove the skin and pit from one avocado and mash with the back of a fork onto a wooden chopping board. Add the chopped garlic and using the fork mash it into the avocado. Squeeze the juice of one lime and incorporate into the avocado and garlic mixture. This tastes delicious as it is, but you might like to add some finely-chopped chilli to add a little heat.

Garlic in Honey

Real honey is a health food all on its own, so adding garlic just makes it even better.

Honey is an antioxidant, and owing to its antimicrobial properties it is effective in treating wounds.

Honey is believed to have anticancer properties, to boost the immune system, it soothes coughs and of course tastes delicious.

Method

1. Peel each clove of garlic and add to a 300 ml jar. The jar should be about three-quarters full, so if the bulbs were smaller you might have to add couple of cloves; if the bulbs were bigger, you might have to take a couple away.

2. Add the honey, ensuring the garlic is completely covered with the honey. The quantity given should be enough, regardless of the size of the cloves.

3. Leave it to ferment for about 5 weeks. After this time the garlic will very likely be ready; however, you can leave it to ferment much longer. Once you are happy with the results, refrigerate.

4. To ensure you get the best result, remember to push the garlic down under the honey to recoat it at least every couple of days.

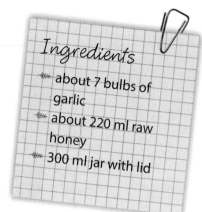

Ingredients

- about 7 bulbs of garlic
- about 220 ml raw honey
- 300 ml jar with lid

Top Tips

- Use as you would fresh garlic.
- Garlic fermented in honey really lends itself well to oriental cooking, so try adding it to your favourite stir-fry.
- Sprinkle chopped honey garlic over salads to add extra antioxidants and depth of flavour.
- Garlic fermented in honey can also be used as an excellent cold remedy – the taste is surprisingly mild and sweet.

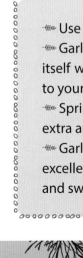

Napa Cabbage Kimchi

Napa cabbage is also known as Chinese leaves, and even though the origins of the vegetable can be found in China, it can now be found growing in the UK.

Napa cabbage is easier to digest than regular cabbage and therefore more suitable for people with digestive disorders. Kimchi is a traditional fermented Korean side dish of which there are numerous varieties.

Method

1. Quarter the cabbage lengthwise, then cut it into chunks of about 5 cm and place in a non-reactive bowl.

2. Add the 2 tbsp of salt and massage well into the cabbage to ensure it is evenly distributed. Cover the bowl with a tea towel and leave for several hours (up to 12 hours).

3. Drain the cabbage in a colander, reserving the brine. Rinse the cabbage and return it to the bowl.

4. Grate the carrots, garlic and ginger. Slice the spring onions into 3 cm lengths.

5. Add the carrots, garlic, ginger, spring onion, remaining salt, hot pepper (or chilli) powder and fish sauce to the cabbage and mix well.

6. Pack the mixture well into a litre jar and top up with the reserved brine if required.

7. Close the jar and open briefly each day to prevent any build-up of gas. Leave for about a week or until it stops bubbling.

8. Refrigerate.

Ingredients

- 1 napa cabbage (about 700 g)
- 1 medium-size carrot
- 2¾ tbsp salt
- 4 spring onions
- 1 thumb-size piece of ginger
- 3 cloves of garlic
- 1½ tbsp Korean hot pepper powder or chilli powder
- 1 tbsp fish sauce
- 1 litre jar with lid

Delicious side dish

Top Tips

- This simple recipe for baechukimchi, the most widely recognised type, gets a three-cabbage rating, as it is time consuming to prepare.
- There are many different kimchi recipe variations, so as you gain confidence feel free to experiment. This is my favourite.
- In Korea, Kimchi is served with every single meal – I even had it served once as a side dish in a pizza restaurant!

Courgette Kimchi

The peel of this diuretic vegetable contains carotenes and magnesium, which accelerate cellular metabolism.

It detoxifies our gut and improves its functionality, while the vitamin A, found in the courgette core, helps in restoring the gut microbiome.

Method

1. Slice the courgettes into coins and place in a non-reactive bowl. Add the 2 tbsp of salt and mix well into the courgette to ensure it is evenly distributed. Cover the bowl with a towel and leave for a couple of hours.

2. Drain the courgettes in a colander, reserving the brine. Rinse the courgettes and return to the bowl.

3. Grate the carrot and ginger and slice the spring onion into 3 cm lengths.

4. Add the carrots, ginger, spring onion, chilli powder, fish sauce and the remaining salt to the courgettes and mix well.

5. Pack the mixture well into the jar and top up with the reserved brine if required.

6. Close the jar, put it into a dark space and open briefly each day to prevent any build-up of gas. Leave for about a week or until it stops bubbling.

Ingredients

- 500 g courgettes
- 1 carrot
- 2¾ tbsp salt
- 1 litre water
- 4 spring onions
- 1 tbsp grated ginger
- 1½ tbsp Korean hot pepper powder or chilli powder
- 1 tbsp fish sauce
- 1 litre jar with lid

Top Tips

- I use my courgette kimchi in salads, but it makes an excellent accompaniment to burgers and hot dogs.
- Try adding a few tablespoons of the courgette kimchi to cold leftover pasta, add a handful of spinach, a cold sliced boiled egg and a drizzle of sesame oil. Top with finely-chopped garlic fermented in honey and serve.

Cucumber Kimchi

Cucumber is not only rich in water, which makes it extremely suitable for diets aimed at weight loss, but its peel contains plenty of vitamin E, which offers protection against free radicals.
It is a detoxifying vegetable.

Method

1. Wash the cucumber well, then chop into cubes (do not peel the cucumber) and place in a non-reactive bowl.

2. Add 1 tbsp of salt and mix in well. Cover and leave for several hours to allow the salt to extract juice from the cucumber.

3. Pour off the excess juice and retain it in case it is needed later.

4. Chop the spring onion into 3 cm lengths and chop the bunch of chives.

5. Grate the garlic and ginger and add them, the spring onion, chopped chives, Korean chilli powder and remaining salt to the cucumber. Mix well and place into a 500 ml jar.

6. Leave the jar in a dark space anywhere from 12–48 hours (depending on your taste preference).

7. Refrigerate and use within a few days.

Ingredients

- 1 large cucumber (about 350 g)
- 1½ tbsp salt
- 1 tsp Korean chilli powder
- 1 clove of garlic
- 1 tsp grated ginger
- 1 tbsp chopped chives
- 1 spring onion
- 500 ml jar with lid

Top Tips

This makes a refreshing accompaniment to chicken satay. Add 1 very finely-chopped chilli, 1 clove of finely-chopped garlic, 1 tsp of medium curry powder, 1½ tbsp of crunchy peanut butter, the zest of half a lime and a dash of low salt soy sauce to a bowl and mix well; thin with a little water if necessary. Chop a skinless and boneless chicken thigh into four equal pieces and cover in half of the satay sauce. Leave for one hour to marinade. You can barbecue the chicken, fry it on the griddle or add it to a thick-based sauce pan to cook. Once cooked through add the remaining sauce. Serve while still warm with three heaping tablespoons of cucumber kimchi.

Curtido

I've provided tried and tested recipes for fermented vegetables rooted in Asia and in Europe; this delicious lightly fermented food, however, has its origins in El Salvador, in Central America.

Method

1. Cut the cabbage into quarters and remove the core. Shred thinly in a food processor or by hand.

2. Grate the carrots and thinly slice the red and the white onion. Place carrots and onions into the bowl with the shredded cabbage.

3. Finely chop the chillies and coriander and add these to the ingredients already in the bowl.

4. Add chilli flakes and salt. Mix all the ingredients together well and cover with a clean dish towel. Leave to rest at room temperature for about one hour to allow the ingredients to release some water.

5. Drain the vegetables and keep the brine in a separate bowl. Add pineapple juice to the brine and mix well.

6. Pack the ingredients into a litre jar and top up with the brine and pineapple juice mixture.

7. Close the lid and leave at room temperature. Curtido will take about 2 to 3 weeks to ferment.

8. Once the jar is open you will have to refrigerate it. It will keep for up to 3 weeks, usually longer if it remains submerged in brine.

Ingredients

- 1 small cabbage (about 1 kg)
- 2 carrots
- ½ red onion
- 4 small white onions
- small bunch of coriander
- 2 chillies
- 1 tsp red chilli flakes
- 1 tsp salt
- 2 tbsp pineapple juice
- 1 litre jar with lid

Curtido will take about 2 to 3 weeks to ferment.

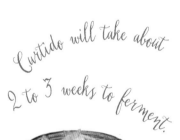

Top Tips

- There are no limits when it comes to ways of using curtido. It works great on its own, as a relish with meat dishes, especially burgers and hot dogs, stirred into a great variety of salads and more.
- If you are looking for something different for dinner, check out the recipe for delicious Salvadoran Pupusas con Curtido (page 150).

Fermented Cauliflower and Carrots

Cauliflower is a member of the cruciferous family, and one serving of cauliflower contains 77 percent of the recommended daily value of vitamin C. It's also a good source of vitamin K, protein, thiamine, riboflavin, niacin, magnesium, phosphorus, fibre, vitamin B6, folate, pantothenic acid, potassium, and manganese.

Method

1. Wash the cauliflower and chop it into small florets.

2. Wash and grate the carrots.

3. Peel and finely slice the garlic.

4. Combine the cauliflower florets, carrots and garlic in a medium-sized bowl. Mix together well, then pack into a 500 ml jar.

5. Dissolve the salt in the water and add to the jar.

6. Close the jar and open briefly each day to prevent any gas from building up.

7. Leave for about two weeks or until it stops bubbling.

Ingredients

- 1 small cauliflower
- 1 or 2 carrots
- 2 cloves of garlic
- 2 tsp salt
- 400 ml water
- 500 ml jar with lid

Top Tips

- This is a really versatile ferment that I love to add to salads. It makes a great probiotic addition to coleslaw or a tasty addition to any cheese board.
- Why not serve this as an accompaniment to seaweed rolls (recipe on page146).
- A wonderful salad can also be made by adding some chopped red onion, capers, fresh chopped parsley, a little Dijon mustard and a dollop of crème fraîche (recipe on page 116). Mix all the ingredients together in a bowl and serve.

Fermented Cherry Tomatoes

Cherry tomatoes contain vitamins B6, folate, thiamine, vitamins A, C, E and K, potassium, manganese, magnesium and a small amount of iron.

The lycopene in tomatoes has been shown to promote the death of malignant prostate cells. Lycopene can also strengthen bones and ward off osteoporosis by slowing the breaking down of bone cells.

Method

1. Wash the tomatoes and place in a non-reactive bowl.

2. Peel and slice the garlic, and along with the mustard seeds, peppercorns and sprigs of dill add to a litre jar.

3. Add the tomatoes on top of the ingredients already in the jar.

4. Dissolve the salt in the water and add to the tomato mixture, leaving about 4 cm of space at the top of the jar.

5. Seal the jar and leave at room temperature, out of direct sunlight for about a week or until bubbling stops. This can be quite a fizzy ferment, so open the jar daily to allow any gas to escape.

6. Once the mixture is fermented to your liking refrigerate.

Ingredients

- 450 g cherry tomatoes
- 3 cloves of garlic
- 1 tsp mustard seeds
- 1 tsp black peppercorns
- several sprigs of fresh dill
- 2 tsp salt
- 1 litre water
- 1 litre jar with lid

Top Tips

- Cherry tomatoes are so easy to ferment. They are simply delicious as they are, but they can be thrown into salads too.
- To make a delicious sauce for pasta, just whizz the tomatoes with some fresh basil and black peper.
- The whizzed up tomatoes can also be used for the tomato juice for the Pickled Mary cocktail (page 154).
- On a warm summer's day, when cherry tomatoes are in season, why not try the delicious recipe for a cool and refreshing gazpacho soup (page 142).

Fermented Celery

Celery simply does not get the credit it deserves. Did you know it is packed full of insoluble fibre, which is excellent for the digestive system?

Celery is also believed to lower bad cholesterol levels in the blood and lower blood pressure, too. Studies have also shown that the luteolin, which celery contains, may help combat some types of cancer.

Method

1. If you have bought a whole bunch of celery, remove the leafy part and separate it into individual stalks. Rinse the stalks well, as often there is a lot of dirt hidden in the bottom joint.

2. Chop the celery stalks into 10 cm lengths and place in a jar along with the whole cloves of peeled garlic.

3. In a small bowl dissolve the salt in the water, then pour over the celery and garlic making sure they are fully submerged.

4. Seal the jar and leave at room temperature for about a week.

5. When fermented to your liking place in the fridge.

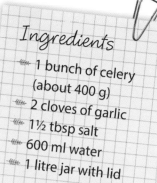

Ingredients

- 1 bunch of celery (about 400 g)
- 2 cloves of garlic
- 1½ tbsp salt
- 600 ml water
- 1 litre jar with lid

Top Tips

- This is a delicious snack on its own, yet it can also be eaten with variety of creamy spreads, like hummus.
- Fermented celery can also be added to salads. For a delicious salad try crumbling some blue cheese into a bowl with chopped fermented celery, add a handful of hazelnuts, the zest of a lemon, 1 tbsp of honey and some cracked black pepper. Mix well together with a dash of olive oil. You can add some dried fruit to add extra sweetness.
- For a great fermented cocktail try a stick in a Pickled Mary (page 154).

Fermented Chillies

The capsaicin in chillies is believed to lower levels of LDL cholesterol and have anti-bacterial and anti-cancer properties. Rich in vitamin C and vitamin A, chillies contain useful flavonoids that can help mop up free radicals in the body. They contain the B-complex vitamins such as niacin, pyridoxine, riboflavin and thiamine. Chillies also contain useful levels of potassium, manganese, iron and magnesium.

Method

1. Slice chillies into rings ½ cm wide.

2. Pack the sliced chillies into a jar, packing tightly, but be sure not to crush them.

3. Dissolve the salt in the water and add to the jar until there is a space of about 2 cm at the top.

4. Ensure the chillies are submerged and close the lid.

5. Leave to ferment for about 6 weeks.

Ingredients

- 500 g chillies
- 250 ml water
- 1 tbsp lemon juice
- 2 tsp salt
- 1 litre jar with lid

Experiment with colours!

- Wear gloves when handling and cutting chillies, and make sure you wash your hands thoroughly with soap after touching them!
- You can use any type of chilli in this recipe. I like to use a mix for a good balance of fruitiness and heat. Experiment to get the right blend for your taste.
- Use this versatile ingredient as you would fresh chilli, but enjoy the extra benefits the fermentation process has created. Try in salads or as a pizza topping once the pizza has been removed from the oven (to preserve the probiotic benefits).

Fermented Bell Peppers

Bell peppers are the only member of the Capsicum family, that do not contain capsaicin, the chemical that gives pepper its hotness – which is why they are often referred to as sweet peppers.

Bell pepper is rich in vitamin C, vitamin E and beta-carotene. The latter gives it excellent antioxidant properties and therefore anti-inflammatory health benefits.

Method

1. Cut the peppers in half and remove the seeds, pith and stalks. Cut each half into about four slices and then cut each slice in half.

2. Roughly slice the garlic and chilli pepper before placing all in a jar along with the peppercorns and tea leaves. The tannin in the green tea will help prevent the peppers from going too soft.

3. Dissolve the salt in the water and add the lemon juice. Pour the brine solution over the peppers and leave to ferment for about two weeks.

4. Check the ferment daily to ensure the mixture stays submerged.

Ingredients

- 3 bell peppers (any colour)
- 1 clove of garlic
- 3 black peppercorns
- 1 chilli pepper (any type)
- 1½ tbsp salt
- 1 tbsp lemon juice
- 600 ml water
- ½ tsp green tea leaves
- 1 litre jar with lid

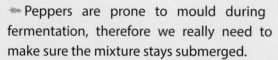 

Top Tips

- Peppers are prone to mould during fermentation, therefore we really need to make sure the mixture stays submerged.
- Chop the peppers up and use them in salads. For a vibrant summer salad, add fermented peppers to a bowl along with avocado, mango, spring onion, a few flakes of chilli, a sprinkling of pumpkin seeds and a simple dressing of honey and lime.
- It is also wonderful in *tabbouleh* or thinly sliced in seaweed rolls.
- Another great way to use fermented peppers is in fermented red pepper hummus. Just blend the fermented peppers with cooked chickpeas, garlic and olive oil.

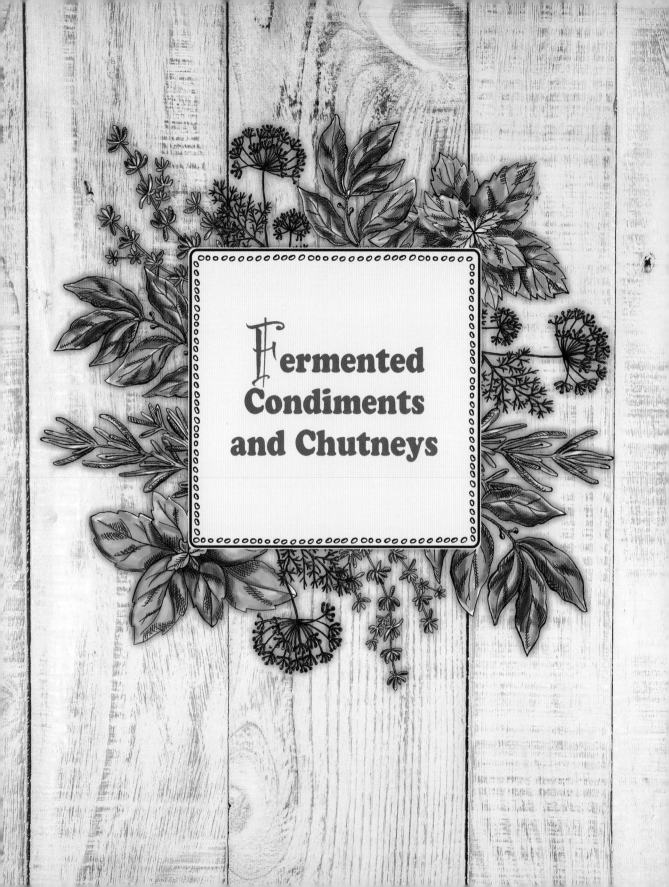

Fermented Condiments and Chutneys

Fermented Piccalilli Inspired Relish

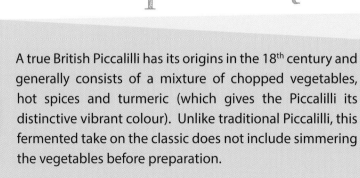

A true British Piccalilli has its origins in the 18th century and generally consists of a mixture of chopped vegetables, hot spices and turmeric (which gives the Piccalilli its distinctive vibrant colour). Unlike traditional Piccalilli, this fermented take on the classic does not include simmering the vegetables before preparation.

Method

1. In a small bowl, make a brine by dissolving the salt in the water, add the lemon juice and leave to one side.

2. Wash the cauliflower, chop it into small florets and place in a large bowl along with the shallots, which should be chopped into 1 cm chunks.

3. Wash and grate the carrot and finely chop the chilli and garlic cloves before also adding to the bowl.

4. Separately, in a small bowl mix turmeric, crushed black peppercorns, cumin seeds, onion seeds, coriander seeds, garam masala and sugar. Combine the spice and sugar mixture with the vegetables and mix well to ensure all the vegetables are evenly coated in the mixture.

5. Pack tightly into a litre jar. Top up with the brine solution and make sure the mixture is submerged.

6. Seal and leave to ferment out of direct sunlight for around two weeks. The spices in this ferment may float to the top of the jar, so check it daily and re-submerge any floating ingredients by pushing them below the brine surface with the back of a clean spoon. This will help to prevent mould growth.

7. Refrigerate when fermented to your liking.

Ingredients

- 1 small cauliflower (about 400 g)
- 1 medium carrot
- 5 shallots
- 2 cloves of garlic
- 50 g light Muscovado sugar
- 1 medium-hot red chilli
- 4 tsp turmeric
- 5 black peppercorns, crushed
- 1 tsp cumin seeds
- 1 tsp onion seeds
- 1 tsp coriander seeds
- 1 tsp garam masala
- 1 tbsp salt
- juice of half a lemon
- 300 ml water
- 1 litre jar with lid

Top Tips

- Play around with your choice of vegetable and use this tasty ferment to liven up cold meats or cheese boards.
- It also makes a delicious topping on hot dogs or burgers, and can be served as an accompaniment to Asian dishes.

Fermented Red Onion Relish

Onions, especially red onions are a great source of the flavonoid quercetin, which is known to have anti-inflammatory, antioxidant and anti-microbial properties.

The greatest amount of flavonoids are found in the outer layers – red onion can lose up to 20 % of its quercetin and 75 % of its anthocyanins if the outer layers are removed.

Method

1. Chop or slice the red onion and place it in a bowl. Add salt, chilli flakes and peppercorns and mix well.

2. Leave to stand for about 10 minutes until the onions begin to release their juices.

3. Pack the ingredients into a litre jar, adding the bay leaf about half way through.

4. Close the lid and leave for 24 hours. If after 24 hours the onions have not released sufficient brine to cover the mixture then prepare and add sufficient brine (1 tsp salt per 120 ml water) to cover.

5. Leave to ferment for 5 to 6 weeks.

Ingredients

- 1 kg red onions
- 1 tbsp salt
- 1 tbsp red chilli flakes
- 5 black peppercorns, crushed
- 1 bay leaf
- 1 litre jar with lid

Top Tips

- This is an extremely versatile ferment that adds a zing to any sandwich or salad.
- It is also delicious on burgers and hot dogs.
- This relish goes really well with cheddar cheese and works nicely on a cheese board with some oatcakes.
- How about in a warm goat cheese salad with some walnuts?

Fermented Hot Chilli Sauce

This is a delicious and straightforward ferment, but I have given it a three-cabbage rating as it is time consuming and involves several steps.

Wear gloves when handling and cutting chillies and make sure you wash your hands thoroughly with soap after handling them!

Method

1. Snip any stems off the chillies, leaving the crown intact.

2. Remove the peel from the garlic cloves.

3. Add the mustard seeds and garlic to a 500 ml jar before packing in the chillies.

4. Dissolve the salt in the water and add to the jar. Leave to ferment for 4–5 weeks until the bubbling has stopped and the chillies have softened.

5. Soften the sun-dried tomatoes in a little of the brine solution overnight.

6. Add drained tomatoes and smoked paprika to the fermented chillies and blend into a puree.

7. Place the puree back in the jar for a couple of days to allow the flavours to develop further.

8. Bottle the mixture or leave it in the jar and refrigerate.

Ingredients

- 350 g mixed chillies
- 1 bulb of garlic
- 1 tbsp mustard seeds
- 50 g sun-dried tomato
- 1 tsp smoked paprika
- 450 ml filtered water
- 2 tsp salt
- 500 ml jar with lid

Top Tips

- You can use any type of chilli in this recipe. I like to use a mix for a good balance of fruitiness and heat, but feel free to experiment to get the blend that's right for your taste.
- To get a smokier tasting sauce, you can oven bake or grill a couple of bell peppers (preferably red) and add them to the combination of tomatoes, smoked paprika and fermented chillies before blending.

Fermented Salsa

Salsa in both, Italian and Spanish is the term for sauce and is not necessarily tomato-based. However, when speaking about salsa in English, we usually immediately associate it with a kind of spicy tomato sauce used in Mexican cuisine. This fermented version of salsa is indeed a fermented variety of the classic Mexican red tomato-based sauce.

Method

1. Chop the tomatoes and onion into small chunks and grate the garlic. Mix them well and place in a large, non-reactive bowl.

2. Chop the coriander and chilli and add to the mix.

3. Add the lime juice, chipotle flakes and salt to the mixture, and combine all the ingredients using a spatula (remember there is a chilli in there, so do not use your hands to mix if not wearing gloves).

4. Add the mix to a 500 ml jar and leave to ferment for three or four days before refrigerating.

5. Fermented salsa is a relatively short-duration ferment, so use it within a week.

Ingredients

- 500 g tomatoes
- 1 small red onion
- 1 large green chilli (choose the variety depending on how hot you like your salsa)
- 2 cloves of garlic
- 1 small bunch of fresh coriander (about 15 g)
- juice of 1 lime
- ¾ tbsp salt
- ¼ tsp dried chipotle flakes or smoked paprika
- 500 ml jar with lid

Top Tips

- This tasty salsa can be used to liven up any of your favourite Tex-Mex dishes.

- It works really well with nachos – add some warm chilli con carne or vegetables cooked in a chilli sauce to an oven-proof dish. Top with unsalted nachos and plenty of cheese. Pop this under the grill until the cheese has melted. Top with salsa, crème fraîche and guacamole. If you like it hot, why not add some extra fermented chilli?

Fermented Berries

Berries are not only an excellent source of fibre but they are also rich in anthocyanins, which are believed to keep the brain healthy and boost cognitive function. They may also have anti-cancer properties, and they help maintain healthy cholesterol levels and a healthy heart.

Method

1. Add the berries to a 500 ml jar and gently press them down to get rid of the air pockets.

2. In a small bowl mix together the honey, salt and whey, and pour the mixture over the fruit.

3. Add enough water to cover the fruit, then cover with a clean kitchen towel and secure with an elastic band.

4. Because some berries are difficult to keep submerged, stir the mixture 2–3 times over a 24-hour period.

5. After about 24 hours the fruit should have soured slightly and be a little carbonated.

6. Once the berries are fermented to your liking, close the jar with a lid and place it in the fridge where it will keep for about 2 months.

Ingredients

- 200 g fresh berries of your choice
- 2 tbsp honey
- ¼ tsp salt
- 2 tbsp whey
- 500 ml jar with lid

Honey and berries are a perfect match.

Top Tips

- There are no limits on the type of berries you choose to ferment.
- Fermented berries can be eaten as they are but they are particularly delicious blended into smoothies, or as a topping on yoghurt or porridge.
- To make almond milk 'ice-cream' all you need to do is blend the berries with some almond milk, maybe add a few teaspoons of honey and incorporate well. Pour into a plastic lunch box, leaving a few centimetres of space at the top. Cover with a lid and place in the freezer for several hours. Take the 'ice-cream' out of the freezer about 20 minutes before serving to allow it to soften a little.

Fermented Peach Chutney

Peaches are not only delicious, but are jam-packed with nutrients such as calcium, potassium, magnesium, iron, manganese, phosphorous, zinc, and copper. They also contain vitamins A, B1, B3 and B6, C, E and K.

Method

1. Peel and chop the peaches. In a large bowl add the peaches and all the remaining ingredients and mix well.

2. Cover the bowl with a clean cloth and leave for an hour to allow the juices to be released.

3. After an hour place all the ingredients in a 500 ml jar and push down gently to ensure the mixture is submerged. Add as much water as required.

4. Close the lid and leave to sit at room temperature for 2 days. Stir once or twice each day.

5. Once the fermentation is complete, place the chutney in the fridge, where it will keep for about 2 months.

Ingredients

- 200 g fresh peaches
- 25 g raisins
- 25 g walnuts
- ¼ tsp cinnamon
- ¼ tsp ginger
- ½ tsp ground cumin
- ½ tsp fennel seeds
- ½ tsp ground coriander
- ¼ tsp white pepper
- 1½ tsp honey
- juice and rind of 1 lemon (lemon needs to be organic)
- 1 tsp salt
- water (as required)
- 500 ml jar with lid

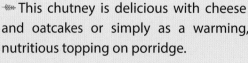

Top Tips

This chutney is delicious with cheese and oatcakes or simply as a warming, nutritious topping on porridge.

Fermented Cinnamon Apples

An apple a day really does keep the doctor away. Apples are full of beneficial nutrients including vitamin C, B–complex vitamins and phytonutrients, which help to combat free radicals. They are also a good source of fibre, calcium, potassium and phosphorous.

Method

1. Wash then slice the lemon and place in a small saucepan with the cinnamon, salt and water. Simmer gently to allow the cinnamon to impart its flavour and the salt to dissolve.

2. Leave to cool, then remove the cinnamon and lemon.

3. In the meantime, wash and thinly slice the apples.

4. Once the liquid has cooled pack the apple slices into a jar, cover with the liquid and wait for about a week.

Ingredients

- 1 lemon (lemon needs to be organic)
- 2 cinnamon sticks
- 2 tbsp salt
- 750 ml water
- 2 medium apples
- 1 litre jar with lid

Top Tips

- These apples go really well with a mild creamy goat cheese, baby spinach and walnuts – just remember you should not need to add any extra salt.
- If you want to give an extra probiotic crunch to fresh coleslaw, cinnamon apples are the perfect answer.
- And to start day with a great healthy meal, just put a spoonful on your hot oatmeal.

Fermented Cranberry Chutney

This recipe is a probiotic twist on a Christmas favourite, but delicious any time of the year. If fresh cranberries aren't available try using the frozen variety.

Cranberries are full of beneficial phytonutrients, and studies have shown that they might help reduce the risk of some 17 different types of cancer, including esophageal, stomach, colon and bladder.

Method

1. Separate the orange into sections, removing any seeds.

2. Blend the orange sections, cranberries, sugar, lemon juice, cinnamon, cloves, ginger, and salt together in a food processor or chop finely.

3. Stir in pomegranate seeds and then pack into a litre jar and cover.

4. Leave to ferment for up to three days. Taste the mixture with a clean spoon each day until soured to your liking.

5. Refrigerate and use within a month.

Ingredients

- 1 large orange
- 1 pomegranate
- 350 g cranberries
- 4 tbsp sugar
- juice of half a lemon
- 1 tsp cinnamon
- 1 tbsp sultana raisins
- 3 cloves
- 1 tsp grated fresh ginger
- 1 tsp salt
- 1 litre jar with lid

Top Tips

- Use up leftover turkey at Christmas by making a seasonal salad with cranberry relish dressing, or top some toasted sourdough bread with warmed turkey and a dollop of cranberry chutney.
- Although cranberries are traditionally thought of as a Christmas food this chutney is too good to keep just for Christmas. Add a dollop to your favourite sandwiches to give them a delicious probiotic twist.
- This relish also works well with most cheeses.

Fermented Mint Dip

Mint is a versatile and aromatic herb believed to be particularly beneficial to those who suffer from irritable bowel syndrome (IBS).

It may also improve the symptoms of headaches, asthma, depression and fatigue. It has even been attributed with improving alertness and memory.

Method

1. Using a food processor or smoothie maker, blend together the mint, coriander, garlic, chilli, ginger, salt and cumin to form a smooth paste.

2. Chop the onion very finely, add it to the mixture together with yoghurt and stir well.

3. Place the mixture in a small jar and cover with a clean cloth secured with an elastic band.

4. Leave the jar at room temperature for 2 days before closing it with a lid and refrigerating.

Ingredients

- 30 g fresh mint
- 15 g fresh coriander
- 1 small onion
- 2 cloves of garlic
- 1 small medium-hot green chilli
- 1 tbsp fresh ginger
- 1 tsp ground cumin
- 1 tsp salt
- 4 tbsp live natural yoghurt (this will be marked on the carton)
- 220–250 ml jar with lid

Fresh, easy to make and tasty.

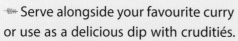

Top Tips

- Serve alongside your favourite curry or use as a delicious dip with crudités.
- This dip can be used as a dressing on your favourite salad.
- I have also used up leftover dip in cooking by using it as a sauce. Try adding spinach, lamb (shallow-fried diced lamb steak) and peas and serve on a bed of steaming brown basmati rice.

Fermented Drinks

Milk Kefir

Milk kefir is believed to have originated in the north Caucasus Mountains in Russia. The word has been in use in the region since at least 1884, but although it is not known when kefir grains first appeared, it is believed they have been in use for thousands of years.

Kefir is very easy to make, but I have given it a three-cabbage rating, as you will have to obtain kefir grains and they need to be looked after.

Method

1. Pour the milk in a litre jar and add the teaspoon of kefir grains.

2. Cover the jar with a clean cloth and secure with an elastic band.

3. Leave for at least 24 hours at room temperature but no longer than 48 hours.

4. Once the kefir has fermented, pour the mixture through a plastic sieve over a plastic bowl. This way you will separate the grains from the liquid. You can reuse the grains as before for your next batch, as they can be reused indefinitely, as long as they are properly cared for.

5. At this stage you can bottle the kefir and pop it into the fridge to be used up within the next week or so. Or alternatively, the kefir can be secondary fermented with the addition of some fruit.

Ingredients

- 1 tsp milk kefir grains
- 1 litre full fat milk
- 1 litre jar
- 1 litre (preferably flip-top) bottle

Tale

- Traditionally kefir was made in goatskin or goatskin bags that were hung near a doorway so that every time someone passed by, the bag would be knocked and agitated ensuring the milk and grains were well mixed.

Milk kefir might contain:

Bacteria
Lactobacillus acidophilus, Lactobacillus brevis, Lactobacillus casei, Lactobacillus delbrueckii, Lactobacillus helveticus, Lactobacillus kefiranofaciens, Lactobacillus kefiri, Lactobacillus paracasei, Lactobacillus plantarum, Lactobacillus rhamnosus, Lactobacillus sake, Lactococcus lactis, Leuconostoc mesenteroides, Pseudomonas fluorescens, Pseudomonas putida and *Streptococcus thermophilus.*

Yeast
Candida humilis, Kazachstania unispora, Kazachstania exigua, Kluyveromyces siamensis, Kluyveromyces lactis, Kluyveromyces marxianus, Saccharomyces cerevisiae, Saccharomyces martiniae and *Saccharomyces unisporus.*

Secondary Fermented Milk Kefir

My favourite is passion fruit, but orange, orange rind, raspberries, strawberries or blueberries also make delicious kefir. Just experiment to find your favourite flavours.

Legend has it that the Caucasian people, known for their longevity, wanted to keep kefir a secret from the rest of the world. At the turn of the 20th century the 'secret' was leaked to Russian officials who wanted the drink to be available to all Russians.

Method

1. Finely chop about 3 tablespoons of the fruit of your choice and put it into an empty bottle.

2. Add the kefir using a plastic funnel and shake gently.

3. Close the lid and leave to stand at room temperature for 12 to 24 hours. The whey might separate a little, but just shake the bottle to mix it back into the mixture.

4. Refrigerate and use within a week.

Ingredients

- 3 tbsp chopped fruit
- 750 ml litre of milk kefir
- 1 litre jar

Top Tips

- The longer milk kefir is left to ferment the more sour it becomes. If left too long the whey will start to separate out and the grains will begin to run out of food. Secondary fermented kefir can be a little fizzy, but this is normal.
- Always use plastic or silicone equipment when working with kefir, as the acidity can cause the metal to leach into the mixture. Wood is porous so not suitable either.
- Kefir grains will multiply, so you can share your extra grains with a friend, eat them, or dispose of them in the food waste bin for composting.

Water Kefir

Less is known about the origins of water kefir but research suggests it may have originated in Mexico. Like milk kefir, water kefir is easy to make, but the grains need a little looking after.

Method

1. Add the sugar and water to a litre jar and stir until the sugar dissolves completely.

2. Add the remaining ingredients and cover with a clean cloth secured with an elastic band.

3. Leave on the counter top at room temperature for 24 hours.

4. After 24 hours, pour the liquid into a non-reactive bowl through a plastic sieve before bottling the kefir by pouring it through a plastic funnel into bottles. This way you will separate the grains from the liquid. You can reuse the grains as before for your next batch, as they can be reused indefinitely, as long as they are cared for.

5. Like milk kefir, you can also secondary ferment your water kefir.

Ingredients

- 2 tbsp water kefir grains
- 65 g sugar
- 2 tbsp organic raisins
- ½ lemon
- 1 slice of fresh ginger
- 750 ml water
- 1 litre jar
- 1 litre (preferably flip-top) bottle

Secondary Fermented Water Kefir

I like to add ginger, but orange and cinnamon also work really well. Just experiment with your favourite fruits or vegetables!

Method

1. Add about 3 tablespoons of the fruit of your choice to a litre flip-top bottle.

2. Add the kefir using a plastic funnel and shake gently.

3. Close the bottle and leave to stand at room temperature for 12 to 24 hours. By this time the liquid should be lightly effervescent.

4. Refrigerate and use within a week.

Ingredients

- 3 tbsp chopped fruit
- 750 ml litre of water kefir
- 1 litre (preferably flip-top) bottle

Water kefir might contain:

Bacteria
Lactobacillus brevis, Lactobacillus casei, Lactobacillus hilgardii, Lactobacillus hordei, Lactobacillus nagelii, Leuconostoc citreum, Leuconostoc mesenteroides, Acetobacter fabarum, Acetobacter orientalis, Stretococcus lactis.

Yeast
Hanseniaospora valbyensis, Lachancea fermentati, Saccharomyces cerevisiae, Zygotorulaspora florentina.

Top Tips

- Be aware that water kefir produces carbon dioxide as it ferments. This gives the kefir its pleasant fizz; however, if left too long there may be a build-up of gas that could cause your bottle to explode or bubble up out of the bottle once opened. For best results, use a flip-top bottle with a rubber seal and do not expose to temperatures warmer than room temperature.
- Kefir grains will multiply, so you can share your extra grains with a friend or dispose of them in the food waste bin for composting.

Kombucha

Kombucha is a fermented tea-based drink believed to have originated in the Far East, probably China, where it has been drunk for at least two thousand years. The first recorded use of kombucha comes from China during the Tsin Dynasty in 221 BC and where it came to be known as "The Tea of Immortality". Making kombucha is a bit of a commitment, as you will have to obtain and care for your SCOBY.

Method

1. Bring the water to a boil, then remove from the heat. Leave to cool for 5 minutes.

2. Add the tea bags to a glass jar and then add the slightly cooled water. Add the sugar and stir well.

3. After 30 minutes, remove the tea bags.

4. Once the liquid has cooled down to room temperature add the starter liquid. Stir well and add the SCOBY. Cover the jar with a clean tea towel and secure with an elastic band and leave in a dark place or fully covered at room temperature for up to 8 days.

5. Taste the brew after about 5 days by inserting a clean straw into the brew and then sealing the end with the pad of your finger. Take the straw and allow the liquid that has drawn up into it to pour into your mouth by releasing your finger from the closed end. It is ready when it has lost the freshly brewed tea smell and is neither too sweet nor too sour.

6. You will notice a new baby SCOBY starting to form on the surface of the brew.

7. When fermented to your liking, with clean hands, remove the SCOBY and the baby SCOBY and place in a clean jar and cover with some of the fermented kombucha. This will now act as your new starter liquid.

8. Bottle the liquid in 500 ml flip-top bottles.

9. The kombucha is ready to drink immediately; however, you can secondary ferment the kombucha to encourage more fizz and to add additional flavour.

Ingredients

- 2 litres water
- 6 organic tea bags (green or black tea)
- 160 g white sugar
- 200 ml kombucha starter (see page 101)*
- SCOBY (see pages 98–99)
- 2 litre jar
- 4 x 500 ml (preferably flip-top) bottles

Secondary Fermented Kombucha

Kombucha spread to Russia, through eastern Europe to Germany and Denmark where its popularity gradually died out.

After the WWII Dr Rudolph Skelnar renewed interest in kombucha in Germany. He used it to treat patients suffering from cancer, diabetes, high blood pressure and metabolic disorders.

When making secondary fermented Kombucha experiment with flavours, and try adding some spices.

Method

1. Before bottling the kombucha add 100 ml of fruit juice or puree of your choice (e.g. your own freshly squeezed juice or shop-bought pure fruit juice) to each of the 500 ml bottles. Add the kombucha and shake lightly to distribute the juice. Leave the bottles at room temperature for 3 to 5 days until they start to fizz.

2. When ready, refrigerate and use within a month.

Ingredients
- 200 ml fruit juice or puree
- 800 ml kombucha
- 2 x 500 ml bottles

> **Top Tips**
>
> ✦ As with any ferment there may be a build-up of carbon dioxide. Do not over ferment secondary fermented kombucha and always open bottles of fermented liquids with care.
>
> ✦ SCOBYs and the starter liquid are living organisms that will die if exposed to high temperatures. Only ever add to your tea mixture once it has fully cooled.
>
> ✦ Every time you brew a new batch of kombucha a new SCOBY will form. This can be used to replace an older SCOBY, placed in the compost or given away to a friend.
>
> ✦ Baby SCOBYs can form also in the bottle – this is normal and harmless. You may also notice some brownish stringy particles, which is also normal and harmless as it is only yeast. This can be filtered out if desired.
>
> * If you purchase a kombucha SCOBY from a reputable seller it should come stored in starter liquid. If you obtain a SCOBY from a friend just ask for a cup full of starter to get you going.

Ginger Beer

This will be the most delicious ginger beer you have ever tasted! Although time consuming, the results are worth the effort and the wait.

In order to make ginger beer you will first have to make a ginger starter, also known as a ginger bug.

This process takes up to a week to complete.

Starter - Ginger Bug

Method

1. Add the water and sugar to a small jar and stir until the sugar is dissolved.

2. Add the ginger and stir well.

3. Cover with a clean cloth and secure with an elastic band. Wrap the jar in a clean towel to insulate and keep near a radiator or in a warm place (around 24 °C).

4. After 24 hours add 1½ tsp sugar and a teaspoon of grated ginger and stir well.

5. Continue this process until the mixture begins to fizz. This can take anywhere from 3–7 days. Once the mixture begins to fizz move on to the next phase.

Ingredients

- 250 ml water
- 1 tsp sugar (plus an additional 1½ tsp sugar per day)
- 1 tsp grated ginger (plus an additional tsp per day)
- small jar

Make the most delicious ginger beer!

From Ginger Bug to Ginger Beer

Ginger has potent anti-nausea properties, making it a favourite in tackling morning sickness in the early stages of pregnancy. It can also be used by cancer patients undergoing chemotherapy. Ginger is an anti-inflammatory and may help lower blood sugar levels and ease symptoms of indigestion.

Method

1. Pour the water into a 2 litre jar and add the sugar and lemon juice. Stir well until the sugar has dissolved.

2. Add 3 tbsp of ginger and half of the ginger starter and stir well. Keep the remaining ginger starter in case it is needed.

3. Cover the jar with a clean cloth and secure with an elastic band. Wrap the jar in a clean towel and keep in a warm place (around 24 °C).

4. Stir the mixture each day, and around day 4 the brew should be starting to bubble. If bubbling has not commenced then add the reserved ginger starter.

5. Once the brew is bubbling well, filter it into a bowl through a plastic sieve and bottle it in three 500 ml flip-top bottles.

6. Leave on the worktop for 3 to 5 days to allow the carbonation to build up.

7. Refrigerate and drink within a month.

Ingredients

- 1½ litres water
- 180 g sugar
- 3 tbsp freshly squeezed lemon juice
- 3 tbsp grated ginger
- ginger starter
- 2 litre jar
- 3 x 500 ml (preferably flip-top) bottles

Top Tips

- As with any ferment there may be a build-up of carbon dioxide. Always open bottles of fermented liquids with care.

Rejuvelac

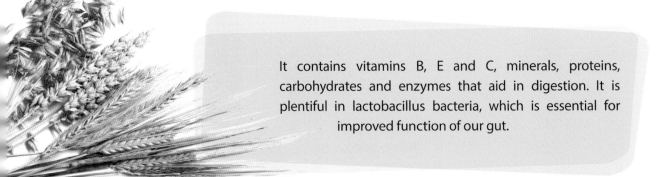

It contains vitamins B, E and C, minerals, proteins, carbohydrates and enzymes that aid in digestion. It is plentiful in lactobacillus bacteria, which is essential for improved function of our gut.

Method

1. Place the grains in a litre jar. Fill with water and cover with a piece of kitchen towel secured with an elastic band. Soak the grains for 24 hours.

2. Drain off the water and leave the grains in the jar, rinsing them two to three times a day until little sprout tails appear.

3. Once the sprouts appear once again fill the jar with water and cover with a piece of kitchen towel secured with an elastic band.

4. Leave for 2 to 3 days until the liquid goes cloudy and begins to bubble.

5. Strain and bottle the liquid, which should taste fresh and lemony.

6. This will keep in the fridge for a week.

Ingredients

- 225 g raw wheat berries or quinoa grains (rye or buckwheat can also be used)
- 1 litre jar
- 1 litre (preferably flip-top) bottle

Top Tips

- As with any ferment there may be a build-up of carbon dioxide. Always open bottles of fermented liquids with care.

Peach Kvass

Kvass is a traditional fermented beverage found throughout Russia, Ukraine, Lithuania, Estonia and Poland, and is most commonly made from rye bread. It may be flavoured with fruits or with herbs such as mint.

This recipe uses raw honey rather than rye bread as a starter. The method is the same for whichever fruit you choose, but fermentation times may vary slightly. Softer fruits will ferment more quickly.

Method

1. Chop the peaches into cubes and add to a litre jar along with the ginger.

2. Dissolve the honey in a glass with some water and add to the jar.

3. Top up the jar with water, leaving 4 cm of space at the top and stir all the ingredients.

4. Cover with a clean cloth secured with an elastic band and leave at room temperature out of direct sunlight for two days or so until the mixture starts to fizz.

5. During this time, stir at least twice a day to distribute the ingredients and to discourage mould.

6. When the mixture is fizzing, filter out the fruit pieces (these can be eaten but will have imparted most of their taste into the liquid). Bottle the liquid in two clean 500 ml flip-top bottles.

7. To increase the fizz you can leave the bottled kvass at room temperature for another day or two before refrigerating.

Ingredients

- 2 peaches
- 1 tbsp raw unfiltered honey
- 1 tbsp coarsely chopped ginger
- filtered water to cover
- 1 litre jar
- 2 x 500 ml (preferably flip-top) bottles

Top Tips

- Plum and cinnamon kvass made the same way is also delicious. Just add couple of chopped up plums and ¼ tsp of powdered cinnamon to the liquid mixture.
- As with any ferment there may be a build-up of carbon dioxide. Always open bottles of fermented liquids with care.

Tepache

The pineapple peel is used to make this delicious, lightly-fermented Mexican beverage, so enjoy the delicious 'leftover' fruit in a kvass or a fruit salad.

Because it is the peel that is being used it is best to try and obtain organic pineapple. If this is not possible then wash the skin well.

Method

1. Wash the pineapple well using a vegetable brush.

2. Remove the top and bottom of the pineapple and peel the fruit leaving 2.5 cm of fruit attached to the peel.

3. Add the water and sugar to a 2 litre jar and stir until the sugar is dissolved.

4. Add the pineapple peelings and stir well.

5. Cover with a clean cloth and secure with an elastic band. Place in a warm place and leave to ferment for up to three days, stirring the mixture at least twice daily.

6. Once the flavour is to your liking, pour the liquid through a sieve into a bowl.

7. Bottle the liquid in four flip-top bottles and leave on the counter top for a further 24–48 hours to allow carbonation to build up.

8. Refrigerate and use within a week.

Ingredients

- 2 pineapples
- 350 g sugar
- 2 litres water
- 2 litre jar
- 4 x 500 ml (preferably flip-top) bottles

Delicious and refreshing

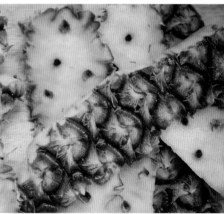

Top Tips

- As with any ferment there may be a build-up of carbon dioxide. Always open bottles of fermented liquids with care.

Fermented Almond Milk

Almond milk is so easy to make and provides a great non-dairy alternative to cow's milk. It has a pleasant nutty taste, a creamy texture and is suitable for vegans and those on a lactose free diet.

Almonds provide a source of vitamins E and B, copper, magnesium, and fibre and are believed to help protect against cancers and cardiovascular disease. This fermented version of course also provides plenty of healthy microbes.

Method

1. Blanch the almonds for 1 minute in freshly boiled water, then drain the almonds and rinse with cold water. Remove the brown skins from the blanched almonds.

2. Dissolve the salt in 750 ml of water.

3. Add the almonds to a litre jar and add the brine. Cover with a clean cloth, secured with an elastic band and leave overnight.

4. Drain the almonds and save the brine in a separate bowl. Blend almonds in a food processor or smoothie maker along with the 550 ml of fresh water, lemon juice, almond extract and honey until smooth.

5. Add the remaining 750 ml of brine and again stir to ensure the ingredients are evenly distributed.

6. Pour the mixture back into a litre jar, close the lid and leave at room temperature for 48 hours.

7. Refrigerate before serving.

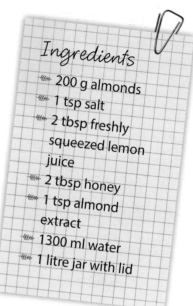

Ingredients

- 200 g almonds
- 1 tsp salt
- 2 tbsp freshly squeezed lemon juice
- 2 tbsp honey
- 1 tsp almond extract
- 1300 ml water
- 1 litre jar with lid

Top Tips

- Fermented almond milk is slightly effervescent and can be used as a replacement for dairy milk.

Other Ferments

Crème Fraîche / Sour Cream

This is a very easy to make ferment that will serve as the perfect accompaniment to any Tex-Mex dish. The fermenting process will consume most of the lactose in the cream and increase its nutrient profile. Use sparingly if you are on a diet, but remember that although this crème fraîche is not guilt-free, it is healthier than its non-fermented counterpart!

Method

1. In a clean bowl mix the cream and kefir.

2. Cover the bowl with a clean cloth and let it stand at room temperature for 48 hours.

3. Once thickened to your liking decant into a sealable jar, refrigerate and leave for another day or two before using.

4. This ferment should keep for several weeks.

Ingredients

- 300 ml double cream
- 5 tbsp milk kefir
- sealable jar

Top Tips

- Use in any recipe that calls for crème fraîche.
- Try adding to salads or any of your favourite Mexican dishes – on top of nachos, quesadillas, chimichangas, tacos, burritos, or as a dip for tortilla chips.
- This also works well with crudités.

Kefir Cheese

I have given this interesting ferment a three-cabbage rating because although this recipe is straightforward it is a little fiddly and time consuming.

Method

1. Place a plastic sieve over a large bowl and insert enough cheese cloth to reach up and over the sides. You can also use a jelly strainer if you have one.

2. Pour the kefir into the cheesecloth-covered sieve and leave to strain for up to 24 hours.

3. Once the whey has strained from the kefir place the solids in a shallow bowl and add a weight to force any remaining whey out. Leave for several hours. Add extra weight if there is any whey remaining.

4. Refrigerate once all the whey has been removed (after about 8 hours).

Ingredients

≪ 500 ml milk kefir
≪ cheesecloth

Top Tips

≪ Use as you would any cream cheese or flavour with herbs and spices.
≪ The whey can be refrigerated and used within a week in recipes that call for a whey starter.

Cultured Butter

Cultured butter is well worth that extra bit of effort and like crème fraîche has an improved nutrient profile compared to its non-fermented counterpart.

Method

1. Add the cream and kefir or live yoghurt to a large bowl and mix with a whisk.

2. Cover the bowl with a clean cloth secured with an elastic band and leave to stand at room temperature for 12–24 hours or until the mixture has thickened slightly and developed a tangy aroma.

3. Refrigerate for 1 hour.

4. Secure a few layers of cheesecloth in a colander and set over a large bowl.

5. Using an electric whisk set on medium, whisk the cream mixture. It will begin to foam, then form peaks before turning grainy, and eventually the butter will separate from the buttermilk. Use a kitchen towel to avoid any splashes.

6. Pour the mixture into the prepared strainer. Once the mixture stops dripping collect up the cheesecloth with the solids within and squeeze it firmly to remove any remaining buttermilk, which can be used for baking.

7. Add some iced water to the cleaned mixing bowl and add the butter. Press the butter with a silicone spatula to encourage further liquid to be released. The water will become cloudy.

8. Pour out the water and replace it with clean iced water and repeat the process until the water remains clear.

9. The butter will become increasingly firm.

10. Once all the liquid has been removed add the salt (if using) and knead in well.

11. Form the butter into a block and store in a butter dish or in greaseproof paper.

12. Cultured butter will keep in the fridge for about 3 weeks.

Ingredients

- 1 litre double cream
- 60 ml kefir kefir or live yoghurt
- some ice
- pinch of salt (optional)
- cheesecloth

Worth all the effort.

Top Tips

- This is truly delicious on a slice of freshly baked sourdough bread.

Sourdough Bread

To make sourdough bread you will first need a starter. You can purchase freeze-dried starter online, obtain it from a friend or make it yourself. If you are making your own starter, this will take about 5 to 7 days.

It can take between one and five days for your starter to begin fermenting, depending on the temperature and environment. If by day 6 you still don't see any bubbling, or the starter smells unpleasant, throw it away and start again.

Sourdough Starter

Method

In order to cultivate sufficient wild yeast to make sourdough bread the mixture will have to be fed daily for 5 to 7 days.

Ingredients
- 100 g plain white flour (plus the same each day for 5 to 7 days to feed)
- 100 ml water (plus the same each day for 5 to 7 days)

Day 1:

In a medium sized non-reactive bowl mix the flour and water and stir well to form a smooth batter. Push any mixture from the sides of the bowl back into the batter.

Cover the bowl with a clean tea towel and secure with a rubber band. Leave to sit at room temperature for 24 hours.

Day 2:

Uncover your bowl and check for bubbles – there may not be any at this stage and this is normal. The starter should begin to smell a little sweet and pleasantly yeasty.

Add the same quantity of flour and water as on day 1 and stir well to form a smooth batter. Push any mixture from the sides of the bowl back into the batter.

Cover the bowl with a clean tea towel and secure with a rubber band. Leave to sit at room temperature for 24 hours.

Day 3:

By today you should see bubbles dotted over the surface of your starter and it should start to smell sour.

Add the same quantity of flour and water as before and again stir well to form a smooth batter. Push any mixture from the sides of the bowl back into the batter.

Cover the bowl with a clean tea towel and secure with a rubber band. Leave to sit at room temperature for 24 hours.

Day 4:

The bubbles should be larger and the batter should have doubled in volume. When the mixture is stirred it should be loose, with a honeycomb texture and plenty of bubbles. If you taste the batter it should be quite sour.

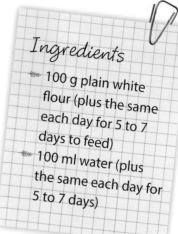

Day 1

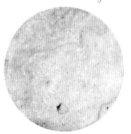

Day 2

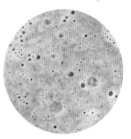

Day 3

Add the same quantity of flour and water as before and again stir well to form a smooth batter. Push any mixture from the sides of the bowl back into the batter.

Cover the bowl with a clean tea towel and secure with a rubber band. Leave to sit at room temperature for 24 hours.

∘∘∘∘ Day 5:

Starter should be ready to use, but continue to feed for another day or two if sufficient bubbles and volume are not yet present.

The batter should have doubled in size since day 4 and should have a bubbly frothy appearance. If you stir the mixture it should feel looser than the day before and webbed with large bubbles. It should taste and smell sour.

If everything is looking, smelling and tasting good, you can consider you starter ripe and ready to use.

Day 5

Looking After Your Starter

Method

Ingredients
- 100 g all-purpose unbleached flour
- 125 ml water

1. Use or discard half of your 'ripe' starter and add the flour and water to the retained half. Mix well until a smooth batter is formed.

2. If you plan to use the starter within the next day or so, then just leave it out on the counter, continuing to 'feed' it daily by discarding half. If it will be longer before you use your starter, cover it tightly and place it in the fridge. You will need to feed it once a week. Once the new flour and water has been added, allow the starter to sit out covered at room temperature to ensure the yeast remains vital.

3. When you are ready to use it again, take it out the night before you are going to be using it.

Cover it tightly.

How to store your starter

If you wish to take a break from making sourdough bread and maintaining the starter you can add 200 g of flour to the starter to make a thick batter. This will provide food for the yeast for long periods in the fridge.

Alternatively you can dry out the batter by smearing it onto a silicon baking mat and leaving it to dry. Once completely dry, crumble the starter into flakes and store it in an airtight container. The sourdough starter can be stored like this for months. To re-start it, dissolve 100 g of the sourdough starter flakes in 100 ml water and add 100 g of flour. Continue feeding the starter until it is active again.

Simple Sourdough Loaf

Method

1. Add the water and sourdough starter to a large bowl and mix together well. Add all the flour and mix until all the ingredients come together.

2. Cover the bowl with a clean damp cloth and let the dough rest for about an hour.

3. Once the mixture has rested for an hour or so add the salt and water mixture and massage it in with your hands to ensure even distribution. Leave covered for a further 10 minutes.

4. After 10 minutes, lift and fold your dough over, do a quarter turn of your bowl and repeat three more times. Repeat 3 times at 30-minute intervals with a final 15-minute rest at the end.

5. Shape the dough lightly into a ball then place in a clean tea towel that has been dusted with flour and place this in a colander to allow air to circulate.

6. Once the dough has doubled in size, place it in the fridge to prove for a further 8 to 12 hours.

7. The following morning preheat your oven to 220 °C (200 °C for fan-assisted ovens) for at least 30 minutes before you are ready to bake. Place a baking stone or baking tray in the oven and a large pan of boiling water underneath. This helps forming a beautiful crust.

8. Once the oven is up to full heat, carefully remove the baking stone or baking tray from the oven and dust it lightly with semolina. Place your dough onto the baking stone or baking tray and mark the top with a sharp knife. Place in the oven and bake for an hour.

9. After one hour, reduce the temperature of the oven to 180 °C and bake for another 10 minutes.

10. Allow to cool fully before slicing. Store wrapped in a clean tea towel.

Ingredients

- 275 ml water
- 100 g sourdough starter
- 100 g stoneground wholemeal flour
- 400 g strong white flour
- 10 g fine sea salt mixed with 15 ml of cold water
- 25 g rice flour mixed with 25 g stone ground white flour (for dusting your proofing bowl)
- semolina to dust the bottom of the baking surface

Fermented Oats

Oats have been shown to reduce bad cholesterol, are high in fibre, and may be beneficial in combating heart disease and fatty liver disease.

Oats are abundant in lignan precursors, which are believed to have anti-cancer properties. Lignans are of particular importance to postmenopausal women.

Method

1. Add the oats, sourdough starter and water to a medium-size non-reactive bowl and stir well.

2. Cover the bowl with a clean tea towel and secure with a large elastic band and leave to sit at room temperature for 2 to 3 days.

3. Make sure to stir the mixture once or twice a day to maintain even distribution.

4. After 2 to 3 days, remove about ¾ of the oats and cook in the normal manner. You can do this by heating gently in a saucepan and adding some more water or milk. Add a little sugar or salt to taste.

5. The remaining oats will serve as your starter for the next batch (use straight away in your next batch or refrigerate in a sealed jar for no more than 2 days, before using as a starter).

6. To begin a new batch, just add 85 g of oats and 60 ml of water to the starter mixture and stir well. Cover your bowl and repeat.

Ingredients

- 280 g rolled oats
- 600 ml filtered water
- 50 g sourdough starter
- pinch of sugar or salt to taste

Top Tips

- Fermented oats are easier to digest as the fermentation reduces the amount of phytic acid. This also means the nutrients within the oats are more bioavailable.
- You can liven up your oatmeal with some fermented berries or a sprinkle of cinnamon.

Fermented Lentils

The humble lentil can reduce the chances of developing type 2 diabetes. This is due to the so-called "second meal effect" – the beneficial effects of eating the lentils (or beans) are still felt many hours after consuming them.

Lentils also help reduce cholesterol levels and blood pressure and the fibre they contain feeds our beneficial gut bacteria, which helps maintain a healthy immune system.

Method

1. Add 115 ml of milk kefir to 600 ml of the water and mix well.

2. Place the lentils in a non-reactive bowl and cover with the water and kefir mixture.

3. Cover with a clean cloth, secure with an elastic band and leave at room temperature overnight.

4. The next day, drain the lentils and repeat the process.

5. Once the lentils are ready, use them as you normally would.

Ingredients

- 400 g lentils
- 230 ml milk kefir
- 1200 ml lukewarm water

Tasty and healthy

Top Tips

If you are short of ideas or lentils are not regularly on your menu, give the Lentil Soup recipe on page 144 a try.

Apple Cider Vinegar

Apple cider vinegar can be made using apple peels and cores or whole apples.

Method

1. In a large clean bowl mix the water and honey until the honey has dissolved.

2. Add the apples to a 2 litre jar and pour the honey water mixture on top.

3. Cover with a clean cloth and secure with an elastic band.

4. Leave at room temperature for about a week, remembering to stir at least twice a day.

5. Once the apple pieces begin to sink, strain the mixture into a large bowl through a plastic sieve.

6. Add the liquid back to the jar and again cover using a clean towel and elastic band.

7. Leave in a warm place for 3–4 weeks. Begin tasting the liquid at 3 weeks and bottle once the vinegar taste is evident.

8. Once the vinegar is ready use within 9 months.

Ingredients

- 2 apples chopped, or the cores and peels of 4 apples
- 1 litre water
- 80 g honey
- 2 litre jar
- 2 x 500 ml (preferably flip-top) bottles

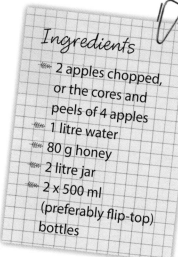

Top Tips

- Research in Japan has shown that taking one to two tablespoons of apple cider vinegar a day can help with weight loss and may help reduce abdominal fat.
- Use this delicious vinegar as you would any regular vinegar, in salad dressings or as a condiment.

Some Great Recipes Using Your Favourite Ferments!

Pork Belly with Kimchi

Serves 4

Pork belly with kimchi is a much-loved combination. Kimchi is also incredibly rich in vitamin C. In Korea, kimchi has been part of the daily diet for over 3000 years and Koreans credit its consumption to good health and longevity.

Method

1. Preheat the oven to maximum temperature (about 220 °C).

2. Finely chop the garlic, slice the onion and roughly chop the mushrooms.

3. To make the marinade, add the kimchi, chilli powder (if using), honey, sugar, garlic, sesame oil and soy sauce to a large bowl and mix well.

4. Using a sharp knife score the pork skin and then add the pork to the marinade, ensuring the meat is coated in the marinade.

5. Remove the pork from the marinade and place it in a heated roasting pan. Place in the oven for 10 minutes (until the skin starts to bubble and brown).

6. In the meantime, add the sliced onions and mushrooms to the marinade along with the water and mix well.

7. Remove the pork from the oven and pour the marinade over the top.

8. Reduce the oven temperature to 170 °C/325 °F/Gas 3.

9. Return the pork to the oven and roast for a further hour until the marinade has become reduced and sticky.

10. Serve with rice.

Ingredients

- 500 g pork belly
- 3 tbsp kimchi
- 2 tsp chilli powder (optional)
- 1 tbsp honey
- ½ tsp brown sugar
- 4 cloves of garlic
- 2 tbsp sesame oil
- 2 tbsp soy sauce
- 1 large red or white onion
- 200 g oriental mushrooms
- 200 ml water

Top Tips

- Pork belly is a boneless cut of fatty meat from the belly of a pig. Choose pork belly that is pale pink in colour and firm to the touch.
- The meat should have an even layer of firm white fat.

Kimchi Bokkeum-Bap

Serves 2

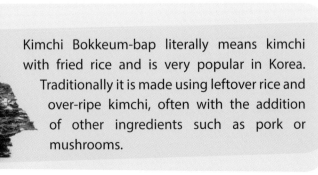

Kimchi Bokkeum-bap literally means kimchi with fried rice and is very popular in Korea. Traditionally it is made using leftover rice and over-ripe kimchi, often with the addition of other ingredients such as pork or mushrooms.

Method

1. Roughly chop the spring onions and garlic.

2. Add some vegetable oil to a hot wok or large frying pan.

3. Add the kimchi and fry for a minute, then add the rice, water, gochujang, spring onions and garlic and cook for about 7 minutes.

4. In the meantime, fry the egg in a frying pan and remove from the heat once the white is cooked but the yolk is still runny.

5. When ready, remove from heat and stir in the sesame oil thoroughly.

6. Serve topped with the fried egg, sesame seeds and flaked nori seaweed.

Add your own favourite vegetables.

Ingredients

- 185 g cooked Korean or Japanese rice
- 200 g kimchi
- 60 ml water
- 2 tbsp gochujang (Korean chilli paste – available in Oriental supermarkets)
- 3 tbsp sesame oil
- 2 spring onions
- 2 cloves of garlic
- 1 tbsp roasted sesame seeds
- 1 sheet roasted nori seaweed (available in most good supermarkets and Oriental supermarkets)
- 1 egg

Top Tips

- Feel free to experiment by adding your own favourite vegetables such as spinach, mushrooms or courgettes, or meat such as chicken, pork or beef.

Kimchi Jjigae

Serves 2 to 3

Kimchi-Jjigae or kimchi stew is probably the most common jjigae or stew in Korea. As with kimchi bokkeum-bap, a longer-aged kimchi is preferred when making this stew.

Method

1. Slice the onions, finely chop the garlic and grate the ginger. Chop the spring onions diagonally and cut the pork into 2 cm cubes.

2. In a deep frying pan, add the kimchi and kimchi brine, the pork, onion, spring onion, salt, sugar, chilli flakes and chilli paste. Cover with the stock and add the sesame oil.

3. Cover and cook for 10 minutes over medium-high heat.

4. Chop the tofu into 2 cm cubes and after 10 minutes give the mixture a stir before adding the tofu on top.

5. Cook for a further 15 minutes.

6. Serve with a side of rice and garnish with finely-sliced spring onion.

Ingredients

- 500 g kimchi
- 60 ml kimchi brine (liquid left over in bottom of kimchi jar)
- 220 g pork belly
- 1 medium onion
- 2 cloves of garlic
- ½ thumb-sized piece of ginger
- 2 spring onions (one for garnish)
- 200 g tofu
- 1 tsp salt
- 2 tsp sugar
- 2 tsp dried chillies (or Korean gochugaru chilli flakes if you can find them)
- 1 tbs gochujang (Korean chilli paste – available from most oriental food stores)
- 1 tsp sesame oil
- 500 ml chicken or fish stock

Top Tips

- This stew is the perfect winter comfort food, but can be enjoyed all year round.
- Instead of pork, try adding chicken or beef to your kimchi jjigae.

Gazpacho

Serves 4

This cold tomato soup has its roots in the Andalusian region of southern Spain. It can be served as a starter, main course, or as a side dish with tapas.

Method

1. Roughly chop the cucumber, tomatoes and spring onion.

2. Deseed and roughly chop the red and green pepper.

3. Finely chop or crush the garlic.

4. Add the chopped ingredients to a bowl along with the white crusty bread and leave to marinade for at least 30 minutes.

5. After 30 minutes, whizz all the ingredients in a blender and season with some freshly ground black pepper.

6. Drizzle in 2 tbsp of the olive oil and 1 tbsp of the sherry vinegar and blend well. Add more olive oil and sherry vinegar, if desired, for taste and a smoother consistency.

7. Chill the gazpacho before serving with some fresh crusty bread.

Ingredients

- 1 cucumber
- 1 red pepper
- 1 green pepper
- 500 g fermented cherry tomatoes
- 500 g fresh tomatoes
- 2 cloves of garlic
- 2 spring onions
- 2 tbsp sherry vinegar
- 75 g stale crusty white bread
- black pepper
- 4 tbsp olive oil

Lentil Soup

Serves 2

Lentils have been used since the stone age. This versatile, beneficial legume is full of minerals, fibre, protein and vitamins, which increase in bioavailability once fermented.

Method

1. Fry the lardons in a tablespoon of oil in a thick-based saucepan until crispy. Remove the lardons from the pan and place in a small bowl on top of a piece of kitchen paper.

2. Coarsely chop the onion and garlic. Add the tablespoon of oil to the bacon fat and fry the onions for a minute before adding the garlic. Fry for a further minute stirring constantly to avoid burning.

3. Chop the carrots and add them along with lentils to the saucepan. Add the spices and cover with ham or vegetable stock. Bring to a boil and let it boil for a few minutes before reducing the heat and allowing the soup to simmer gently for about 20 minutes or until all the ingredients have softened.

4. If you prefer a smooth soup then remove it from the heat and blend until smooth.

5. Serve garnished with a teaspoon of coconut oil and a sprinkle of finely-chopped spring onion.

Ingredients

- 80 g lardons
- 1 large onion
- 2 cloves of garlic
- 2 carrots
- 400 g fermented lentils
- 1 litre ham or vegetable stock
- ½ tsp salt
- ½ tsp black pepper
- 2 tsp garam masala
- 2 tbsp coconut or vegetable oil
- 1 spring onion for garnish (optional)

Seaweed Rolls

Makes 5 rolls (serves 2 or 3)

History is conflicted over which came first, Japanese sushi or Korean kimbap, but both are equally delicious. Japanese tend to add rice vinegar to the rice, whereas Koreans tend to add sesame oil.

Method

1. Place the rice in a large bowl, add 2 tbsp of the sesame oil and mix well.

2. Chop the fermented carrot batons into matchsticks, cut the fermented asparagus into quarters lengthways and thinly slice the avocado.

3. Place the carrots, asparagus and avocado on a large plate.

4. Blanch the spinach by setting it in boiling water for a few seconds. Remove the spinach from the hot water and run it briefly under cold water.

5. Grate the garlic. In a small bowl combine the spinach, garlic, ¼ tsp salt and ½ tbsp of the sesame oil and set on a plate beside the carrots and asparagus.

6. Beat the eggs in a small bowl and add the remaining salt.

7. Heat the vegetable oil in a large frying pan and add the egg, ensuring it covers the surface of the pan.

Ingredients

- 5 sheets sushi grade seaweed
- 1 kg warm cooked rice (about 500 g dry weight)
- 300 g spinach
- 3 cloves of garlic
- ½ tsp salt
- 130 g fermented carrots
- 3 fermented asparagus spears
- ½ avocado
- 3 eggs
- 2 tsp Korean or Japanese soy sauce
- 2½ tbsp sesame oil
- 1 tbsp vegetable oil

8. When the bottom of the egg is cooked remove the pan from the heat and let the omelette cook slowly for about 5 minutes. The omelette should be yellow in colour with little or no browning.

9. Allow the omelette to cool and then cut it into 1½ cm-wide strips. Place the strips next to the other prepared ingredients.

10. If you are using a rolling mat, place a sheet of sushi seaweed on the mat with the shiny side down. Using a metal spoon, cover the seaweed thinly and evenly with some of the rice, leaving about 5 cm clear at the end of the seaweed.

Great at picnics or in lunch boxes!

These seaweed rolls can be shaped by hand, but if you can find a bamboo sushi rolling mat it will make things much easier.

11. In the centre of the rice, place a line of each ingredient along the full width of the seaweed.

12. Using both hands, take hold of the mat and pull it upwards and forwards causing the seaweed to roll over on itself and continue to roll until the seaweed roll is formed.

13. Place the roll seam side down on a plate and repeat the same procedure for the remaining rolls.

14. If you do not have a mat, place the seaweed shiny side down on a clean surface and once the rice and fillings have been added, lift the rice covered end of the seaweed and roll it down tightly onto itself. Continue to roll the entire length of the seaweed.

15. Once the rolls have been made and allowed to sit for a few minutes to seal, cut them into discs of about 1½ to 2 cm.

16. Dip into soy sauce before eating.

Top Tips

⫷ Seaweed rolls (called kimbap in Korea) are great at picnics or in lunch boxes. You can add any ingredient you want to a seaweed roll. Try adding cheese, kimchi or sauerkraut.

⫷ For extra fibre, try using equal portions of white and wholegrain rice, or for a more colourful result, try Korean multigrain rice if you can find it.

Salvadoran Pupusas con Curtido

Makes 8 Pupusas (serves 2 or 3)

Pupusas are a special type of tortilla, traditionally made in El Salvador. They are especially tasty when filled with cheese and are usually served with spicy curtido and salsa.

Method

1. In a mixing bowl combine the masa harina, salt and water and knead to form smooth, moist dough. If the mixture is too dry, add a little more water; if the mixture is too sticky, add a little more masa harina. Cover the bowl with a clean towel and let rest for 10 minutes.

2. With lightly oiled hands, form the dough into 8 balls about 10 cm in diameter. Press your thumb into the centre of each ball to form an indentation. Fill the indentation of each ball with 1 tablespoon of cheese and seal by wrapping the dough around the filling.

3. Gently flatten each ball to form a round disk about ½ cm thick, making sure the filling does not leak.

4. Heat a lightly oiled, thick-based frying pan over medium-high heat. Fry the pupusas for 2 to 3 minutes on each side until golden brown.

5. Serve while still warm with curtido on the side.

Ingredients

- 250 g masa harina (type of corn flour)
- pinch of salt
- 250 ml cup warm water
- 230 g mozzarella (or other cheese of your choice)
- vegetable oil for frying

Top Tips

- Alternatively, pupusas can be filled with meat, fish or vegetables.

Fermented Cocktails

Pickled Mary

Ingredients

- 2 crushed ice cubes
- 2 measures of vodka
- juice of ½ lemon
- 6 dashes of Worcestershire sauce
- ¼ tsp fermented chilli sauce
- 150 ml tomato juice (blended fermented tomatoes)
- pinch of smoked sea salt
- pinch of freshly ground black pepper (you can use white pepper if you prefer)
- stick of fermented celery and other vegetable/fruit (optional) to garnish

Method

1. Add the ice, then the vodka to a tall narrow glass.

2. Add the lemon juice, Worcestershire sauce, chilli sauce and tomato juice and stir well.

3. Season with the salt and pepper and garnish with the fermented celery stick.

4. Serve straight away.

Tepache Colada

Method

1. Put the glass that you will use for serving the tepache colada into the freezer for about ten minutes.

2. Place all your ingredients into a blender (apart from the garnish) and blend until smooth.

3. Pour into a chilled or frozen glass and add the garnish.

4. Serve straight away.

Ingredients

- 6 or 7 chunks of pineapple and a wedge to garnish
- 1 tsp sugar
- 1 tbsp coconut cream (you can use 25 ml of fresh or fermented coconut water if you prefer)
- 50 ml white rum (Bacardi or other)
- 50 ml freshly brewed tepache or pineapple kefir
- crushed ice

Best served cold!

Cranberry Gin Fizz

Method

1. Make your regular water kefir. In the secondary fermenting phase add 100 ml of cranberry juice per 1 litre of kefir (see page 96).

2. Add the crushed ice to a glass, then add the gin and lemon juice.

3. Pour over the cranberry water kefir and add a dash of sparkling water if you need a bit of extra fizz. Add two thin lime slices and a teaspoon of cranberries to garnish.

4. Serve straight away.

Ingredients

- 2 crushed ice cubes
- 60 ml gin
- 2 tbsp fresh lemon juice
- 240 ml cranberry water kefir
- dash of sparkling water (optional)
- garnish (optional)

Christmas Daiquiri

Method

1. Make your regular water kefir. In the secondary fermenting phase add the juice of three or four clementines per 1 litre of kefir and a stick of cinnamon or ½ tsp cinnamon powder (see page 96).

2. Shake all the ingredients in a cocktail shaker with ice cubes, then strain into a cocktail glass. Add a little cinnamon powder and a cinnamon stick to garnish.

3. Serve straight away.

Ingredients

- 2 or 3 ice cubes
- 50 ml Bacardi 8-Year Old Rum
- 25 ml clementine and cinnamon water kefir
- 1 tsp maple syrup
- cinnamon stick and a pinch of cinnamon powder, to garnish

To warm you up!

Key Literature and Sources

Blythman J., *Swollow This: Serving Up the Food Industry's Darkest Secrets*, Fourth Estate, 2015.

Chikezie P. C., Ojiako O. A., Czanide and Aflatoxin Loads of Processed Cassava (Manihot eculenta) Tubers (Garri) in Njaba, Imo State, Nigeria, *Toxicology International*, September 2013, 20 (3), pp. 261–267.

Collen A., *10 % Human: How Your Body's Microbes Hold teh Key to Health and Happines*, William Collins, 2015.

Greger M., *How Not to Die: Discover the Foods Scientifically Proven to Prevent and Reverse Disease*, Macmillan, 2016.

Handbook of Fermented Functional Foods, Functional Foods and Nutraceuticals, Second Edition, ed. Farnworth E. R., CRC Press, 2008 (2003).

Hui Y. H. et al., *Handbook of Food and Beverage Fermentation Technology*, CRC Press, 2004.

Jayabalan R. et al., A Review on Kombucha Tea – Microbiology, Composition, Fermentation, Beneficial Effect, Toxicity, and Tea Fungus, *Comprehensive Reviews in Food Science and Food Safety*, 13/4, July 2014, pp. 538–550.

Katz S. E., *The Art of Fermentation*, Chelsea Green Publishing, 2012.

Katz S. E., *Wild Fermentation*, Chelsea Green Publishing, 2003.

Kitabake N. et al., Traditional non-alcoholic beverage, Togwa, in East Africa, produced from maize flour and germinated finger millet, *International Journal of Food Sciences and Nutrition*, November 2003, 54 (6), pp. 447–455.

Mugula J. K. et al., Microbiological and fermentation characteristics of togwa, a Tanzanian fermented food, *International Journal of Food Microbiology*, 2003, 80, pp. 187–199.

Useful Websites

www.bbcgoodfood.com

www.culturesforhealth.com

www.fao.org

www.foodandnutrition.org

www.greenmedinfo.com

www.healthguidance.org

www.hmpdacc.org/ (NIH Human Microbiome Project)

www.news.aces.illinois.edu

www.nourishkefir.co.uk

www.seedsofhealth.co.uk

www.thenourishinggourmet.com

www.wildfementation.com (Sandor Katz's official website)

Photographic Credits

Shutterstock, apart from the following:

Page 24 (top) © Rachel Mulligan

Page 30 © Mina Mušinović

Page 38 (top) © Ksenija Konvalinka

Page 43 (left) © Rachel Mulligan

Page 44 (top) © Rachel Mulligan

Page 47 (bottom right) © Rachel Mulligan

Page 55 © Rachel Mulligan

Page 65 (right) © Rachel Mulligan

Page 73 (left) © Rachel Mulligan

Page 75 (bottom) © Rachel Mulligan

Page 77 (center) © Rachel Mulligan

Page 93 (right) © Rachel Mulligan

Page 107 (left, center) © Rachel Mulligan

Page 109 © Rachel Mulligan

Page 119 (bottom right) © Rachel Mulligan

Page 123 (top) © Rachel Mulligan

Page 133 (top) © Rachel Mulligan

Page 136 (top) © Rachel Mulligan

Page 139 © Rachel Mulligan

Page 146 (top) © Ksenija Konvalinka

Page 147 © Ksenija Konvalinka

Page 148 (top) © Ksenija Konvalinka

Page 149 © Ksenija Konvalinka